Acknowledgements

Thanks go out to my co-host Aaron van Wirdum for helping me explain the technical stuff in my head. Similarly, my editor Natalye Childress[1] helped me clarify things even more by transforming the podcast episodes to chapters and asking lots of clarifying questions.

Thanks to Bitcoin Magazine for editing, publishing, promoting, and later even rebranding the podcast.

Ruben Somsen was a co-host for several episodes, including one that made it into the book.

Michael Folkson wrote several of the transcripts for the Taproot activation episodes.

The episode show notes were written by Aaron. They form the basis of appendix A, which describes episodes not covered in the book.

Thanks to Martin Zumsande and others for feedback on earlier drafts.

Finally, thanks to all the Bitcoin Core developers and other volunteers who work to make Bitcoin a success and make my life interesting.

---

[1] https://natalye.com

Contents

Bitcoin: A Work in Progress
Technical innovations from the trenches

Sjors Provoost

Bitcoin: A Work in Progress
Technical innovations from the trenches

Paperback First Edition April 2022
v1.0: April 2022

Published by Purple Dunes
ISBN 978-90-9036042-3

Email		sjors@sprovoost.nl
Blog		https://sprovoost.nl/
Twitter		@provoost
Mastodon		https://m.sprovoost.nl/@sjors
Book source		https://btcwip.com/source

PGP fingerprint:
ED9B DF7A D6A5 5E23 2E84 5242 57FF 9BDB CC30 1009

Part I

The Basics

Overview

In this part, we explain a number of basic concepts that will be referred to in later chapters. For a more thorough and structured introduction to Bitcoin, consider reading *Mastering Bitcoin* by Andreas M. Antonopoulos,[2] or *Grokking Bitcoin* by Kalle Rosenbaum.[3] However, these books aren't required reading to follow along with this book.

In chapter 1, we explain how a Bitcoin address isn't something that exists on the blockchain, but rather is a convention used by wallet software to communicate where coins must be sent. We also explain how these addresses are encoded using base58, and more recently with bech32.

In chapter 2, we explain how, the very first time your Bitcoin node starts up, it finds peers to communicate with. You'll also get a primer on Tor.

Chapter 3 explains the 2017 SegWit soft fork and talks about how it increased the block size and paved the way toward the Lightning network by solving transaction malleability.

Finally, chapter 4 explains what libraries are, how they cause problems, and what happened with OpenSSL in particular.

---

[2]https://www.oreilly.com/library/view/mastering-bitcoin/978149
1902639/

[3]https://www.manning.com/books/grokking-bitcoin

Reading Hints

Each chapter contains a QR code that takes you to the corresponding podcast episode and its show notes. The episode number is shown below the QR code. You can also find the episode in your favorite podcasting application by searching for *Bitcoin, Explained*. Or, play it in your browser.[4]

There is a tiny QR code displayed next to each URL. These go through btcwip.com in order to keep them small. We won't track you.

Throughout the text, there are many references to the Bitcoin Core node software and its built-in wallet. Appendix B has some screenshots of it and shows a typical workflow for sending and receiving bitcoin.

---

[4]https://nadobtc.libsyn.com

Chapter 1

Bitcoin Addresses

Ep. 28

Bitcoin addresses aren't part of the Bitcoin blockchain; rather, they're conventions used by Bitcoin (wallet) software to communicate where coins must be sent to: either a public key (P2PK), a public key hash (P2PKH), a script hash (P2SH), a witness public key hash (P2WPKH), or a witness script hash (P2WSH). Addresses also include some metadata about the address type itself.

Bitcoin addresses communicate these payment options using their own numeric systems, and this chapter will break down what these different systems mean. It'll also delve into some of the benefits of using Bitcoin addresses in general and bech32 addresses specifically. We explain how the first version of bech32 addresses included a (relatively harmless) bug, and how it was fixed. We finish the chapter with some quantum talk.

Some History

When you send bitcoin to someone, you're creating a transaction that has several inputs and at least one output. The output specifies who can spend it by putting a constraint on it — a fancier term for constraint is encumbrance.[1]

The most trivial encumbrance is that anybody can spend the coin. That's not a good idea, because it'll be stolen very quickly. So in the early days, most coins on the blockchain were encumbered in one of two ways: Pay-to-Public-Key (P2PK) and Pay-to-Public-Key-Hash (P2PKH). The first can be read as "only the holder of the private key corresponding to the public key X may spend this coin," and the second as "only the holder of the private key corresponding to a (secret) public key, which hashes to X, may spend this coin."

Back then, it was possible to send bitcoin to people's IP addresses,[2] but this feature was dropped in 2012. When this was possible, you could connect to someone's IP address and ask for a public key, and the person would give you their public key.[3] Your wallet would then create a new coin encumbered with a P2PK script.

Today, this workflow might seem strange,[4] but it matches the then-common pattern of peer-to-peer apps like Napster or Kazaa, where you'd connect directly to other people and download things from them. Nowadays, you probably don't know the IP addresses of your friends, and they might even change all the time when they're on mobile devices. Although you can instruct your Bitcoin node to specifically connect to a friend's node, it typically just connects to random peers (see chapter 2).

---

[1]https://www.oreilly.com/library/view/mastering-bitcoin/978149 1902639/ch05.html#tx_script

[2]https://en.bitcoin.it/wiki/IP_transaction

[3]For the curious code archaeologist: On the sender node there was a UI dialog that prompted for an amount and IP address. The function `StartTransfer()` created a blank cheque transaction, into which `checkorder` on the recipient node would insert a P2PK script (as the `scriptPubKey`). `OnReply2()` would then insert the amount, sign the transaction, return it to the recipient and also broadcast it. https://github.com/bitcoin/bitcoin/blob/v0.1.5/main.cpp#L2004-L2042

[4]And unsafe, as Satoshi acknowledged: https://bitcointalk.org/index.php?topic=158.msg1322#msg1322

The more common way of doing transactions is similar to how bank transfers work. Someone provides you with an address and you send coins to it, just as you'd send money to a bank account number. This initially always used P2PKH, as we'll explain below.

Instead of sending a transaction directly to the recipient, it makes its way through all the nodes on the network, eventually to be seen by a miner node, which includes it in a block. Your counterparty may see the transaction as their node receives it from one of its peers, or they'll see it once they receive the block it's in.

A third way of doing transactions is to mine bitcoin, which involves sending the block reward to yourself. In the beginning, Bitcoin had a piece of mining software built into the software, so if you downloaded the Bitcoin software, it would just start mining. It would then send coins to your own wallet, so there was no need to communicate an address. Those coins were encumbered with P2PK.[5]

So What Is an Address?

An address is a convenient way to communicate which script needs to go on the blockchain. As we said above, the purpose of this script is to constrain the coin so that only the recipient can spend it.[6] The address itself doesn't exist on the blockchain. It doesn't even contain the full script.

---

[5]Why did Satoshi's initial version support both P2PK and P2PKH? We're not sure. The P2PK way of paying someone was only ever really used for paying to an IP address, and for the miner, the block reward. Neither needed human interaction. In scenarios that did involve human interaction, P2PKH was used. When using an address, P2PKH, and not P2PK, is implied. Automated systems don't require the concept of an address, since they can just as well handle script, and so there's no such thing as a P2PK address.

[6]So far, the analogy to bank accounts holds, but we'll learn in chapter 10 that scripts can be far more powerful than just functioning as buckets to hold money for their owners.

Of the two main types of scripts in use back in the day, addresses were only used for Pay-to-Public-Key-Hash (P2PKH). When a wallet sees this address, it produces a script for the Bitcoin blockchain, which requires that the person spending it has the public key belonging to the hash (chapter 10 contains the actual script). Only the hash is published, so the public key remains secret until the recipient spends the coins.

An address starts with the number 1, followed by the hash of the public key. It's encoded using something called base58. Here's an example: 1HLoFgMiDL3hvACAfbkDUjcP9r9veUcqAF

Base Systems Explained

To understand what base58 is, it's important to first understand more about base systems in general.

With base10, think about your hand. You have 10 fingers. So if you want to, for example, express the number 115 (1, 1, 5), you can make three gestures with your hands by showing 1, 1, and 5. That's also how you write down numbers, which — since the invention of clay tablets and paper — is more convenient than using fingers. So base10 is a decimal system that uses 10 different symbols, in various combinations, to represent any number (integer).

However, there have been — and still are — different bases. For example, the Babylonians[7] used base60. And to read machine code, typically you'd use hexadecimal,[8] which is base16 — 0 to 9, and then A to F. Meanwhile, computers tend to use base2 internally — a binary number system — because transistors are either on or off. This translates to

---

[7]https://blogs.scientificamerican.com/roots-of-unity/ancient-babylonian-number-system-had-no-zero/

[8]https://en.wikipedia.org/wiki/Hexadecimal

using two digits, either 0 or 1, to do everything, and you can express any number that way.

Satoshi introduced[9] base58, which uses 58 different symbols: 0 through 9, and then most of the alphabet in both lowercase and uppercase. But there are some letters and numbers that are skipped because they're ambiguous and users could easily mistake them for the wrong one — for example, the number 0 and the uppercase letter O, and capital I and lowercase l.

Have you ever seen email source code for an attachment or similar? There are a lot of weird characters. That's base64, and base58 is based on that. But base64 includes characters like underscores, plus, equals, and slash. These are omitted in base58 to make visual inspection easier and to behave nicely as part of a URL.

Base58 and the Pay-to-Public-Key-Hash

So how does this relate to P2PKH? Well, the address is expressed as a 1, followed by the public key hash, which is expressed in base58.

That's the information you send to somebody else when you want them to send you bitcoin. You could also just send them 0x00,[10] and then the public key. And maybe they'd be able to interpret that, but probably not.

In theory, you could send somebody the Bitcoin script in hexadecimal, which is the format used on the blockchain, because that's just binary information. The blockchain has this script that says, "If the person has the right public key hash and the public key belonging to this public key hash,

---

[9]https://tools.ietf.org/id/draft-msporny-base58-01.html

[10]A pair of hexadecimal digits, prefixed by 0x, is often used to denote bytes, which contain $16 \times 16 = 256$ bits, so this represents one byte with the value 0.

then you can spend it." To learn more about how Bitcoin scripts work, refer to chapter 10.

But even with all these options, the convention is that you use this standardized address format, which explains why all traditional Bitcoin addresses start with a 1, and why they're all roughly the same length.

In addition to using base58 for sending a Bitcoin address, you can also use it to communicate a private key. In such a scenario, the leading symbol is a 5, which represents 128. That's then followed by the private key.

In the past, users had paper wallets they could print. And if they were generated securely without a back door, then on one side of the piece of paper would be something starting with a 1, and on the other side of the paper would be something starting with a 5. And then it specified that only the Bitcoin address should be shown, but the private key shouldn't be shared.

There are also addresses that begin with a 3, which is for coins encumbered by the hash of a script, rather than the hash of a public key. We'll cover Pay-to-Script-Hash (P2SH) in chapter 10. Usually these are multi-signature addresses, but they could also be SegWit addresses.[11]

Although base58 addresses worked fine, there was room for improvement. And this came in the form of bech32.

---

[11]As explained in chapter 3, SegWit typically uses bech32 addresses. But it took a long time for all wallets and exchanges to support sending to bech32 addresses. To still take advantage of some of SegWit's benefits, an address type that looks like regular P2SH to the sender was introduced, but it contains SegWit magic under the hood. This is called a P2SH-P2WPKH address: https://bitcoincore.org/en/segwi t_wallet_dev/

Along Came Bech32

In March of 2017, Pieter Wuille spoke about a new address format,[12] bech32, and it's been used since SegWit arrived on the scene. As the name suggests, it's a base32 system, which means you have almost all the letters, and almost all the numbers, minus some ambiguous characters that you don't want to have because they look too much like other numbers or letters.

One of the biggest differences between bech32 and base58 is that there isn't a mixture of uppercase and lowercase letters. Instead, each letter is only in there once — either in all uppercase or all lowercase — which makes reading things out loud much easier. The precise mapping of which letter or number corresponds to which value is, like in base58, fixed but arbitrary: The fact that P means 0 and Q means 1 has no deeper meaning.

Table 1.1: Bech32 mapping. E.g. q means zero, 3 means 17 (1 + 16)

	0	1	2	3	4	5	6	7
+0	q	p	z	r	y	9	x	8
+8	g	f	2	t	v	d	w	0
+16	s	3	j	n	5	4	k	h
+24	c	e	6	m	u	a	7	l

A bech32[13] address consists of two parts separated by 1, e.g. `bc1q9kdcd08adkhg35r4g6nwu8ae4nkmsgp9vy00gf`.

The first part is intentionally human readable, e.g. "bc" (Bitcoin) or "lnbc" (the Lightning network on Bitcoin). The values represented by "b," "c," etc. have no meaning. Rather, they're there so humans can recognize, "OK, if the address starts with bc, then it refers to Bitcoin as the currency."

---

[12] https://www.youtube.com/watch?v=NqiN9VFE4CU

[13] Bech32 spec (BIP 173): https://en.bitcoin.it/wiki/BIP_0173

However, wallets will look for the presence of these values as a confidence check, and it's included in the checksum.

The 1 is just a separator with no value. And if you look at the 32 numbers, 1 isn't included — it means "skip this."

The second part starts with the SegWit version number. Version 0 is represented with Q (bc1q...) — see chapter 3. Version 1 is what we call Taproot (see part V), as it's represented with "P" (bc1p...). For version 0 SegWit, the version number is followed by either 20 bytes or 32 bytes, which means it's either the public key hash or the script hash, respectively. And they're different lengths now, because SegWit uses the SHA-256 hash (32 bytes) of the script, rather than the RIPEMD160 hash (20 bytes) of the script.

In base58, the script hash is the same length as the public key hash. But in SegWit, they're not the same length. So by looking at how long the address is, you immediately know whether you're paying to a script or you're paying to a public key hash. As an aside, Taproot removes this length distinction, thereby slightly improving privacy.

So the new part is that there's a set of 32 characters, but otherwise, things are very similar to base58. It's again saying, "OK, here's a P2PK address." In this case, it's a Pay-to-Witness-Public-Key-Hash (P2WPKH), where witness refers to SegWit, but it's the same idea. There's a short prefix that tells both humans and the computer what the address is about, and this is followed by the hash of the public key or script.

Thirty-Two Dimensional Darts

However, conciseness isn't the only benefit here. Another is error correction, or at least detection.

If there's a typo in an address, then in the worst case scenario, you're sending coins to the wrong hash of a public key. When the recipient tries to spend the coin, they reveal the public key, but due to the typo, its hash won't match what the blockchain demands. The coins are forever lost.

Fortunately, base58 addresses contain a checksum at the end. That way, if you make a typo, the checksum at the end of the address won't work. Your wallet will alert you to this, and it'll refuse to send the transaction (the blockchain won't protect you; only your wallet will, hopefully). But if you're really unlucky, a typo can be such that it produces a correct checksum by sheer coincidence.

Bech32 was designed in such a way to make such a disastrous coincidence extremely unlikely. In addition, it won't just tell you that there *is* a typo; it can tell you *where* the typo is. This is determined by taking all the bytes from the address and then hashing it using some sophisticated mathematical magic.[14] You can make about four typos and it'll still know where the typo is and what the real value is. If you do more than that, it won't.

To illustrate this conceptually, it's like if you have a wall and you draw a bunch of non-overlapping circles on it. The bullseye of each circle represents a correct value, whereas any other spot within the circle represents a typo. If you're a good dart player, most of the time you'll hit the bullseye, i.e. you typed the correct value. If you slightly miss the bullseye but you're still within that big circle, the value will be slightly incorrect. Error *detection* is knowing that you missed the bullseye. Error *correction* is the equivalent of moving the dart to the nearest bullseye.

The idea there is you want the circles to be as big as possible, to facilitate even the sloppiest dart thrower, but you don't want to waste too much space. Similarly, we don't want Bitcoin addresses to be hundreds of characters long. That's the kind of optimization problem mathematicians love.

---

[14]Math behind bech32 addresses: https://medium.com/@MeshCollider/some-of-the-math-behind-bech32-addresses-cf03c7496285

In the case of bech32, instead of a two-dimensional wall, you have to somehow imagine a 32-dimensional "wall" with 32-dimensional hyperspheres. You're hitting your keyboard, and somewhere in that 32-dimensional space, you're slightly off, but you're still inside this hypersphere, whatever that might look like. In that case, your wallet knows where the mistake is, and it prevents you from sending coins into the ether.[15]

But... There's a Problem

In 2019 it was discovered that, if a bech32 address ends with a P, then if you accidentally add one or more Qs to it, it still will match the checksum, and you won't be told there's a typo. In turn, your software would think it's correct, you'd be sending money to the wrong address, and it would be unspendable, as we explained above.

The good news is that bech32 was only used for SegWit, and SegWit addresses were constrained — they had to be either 20 bytes or 32 bytes. So luckily, if you add another Q to a 20- or 32-byte address, then its length would be invalid. Your wallet would detect this and refuse to send coins. A similar size constraint was considered for Taproot, but thanks to the solution below, it wasn't needed. A flexible length makes future improvements to Taproot easier.

---

[15]Pardon the pun, but early Ethereum wallets didn't use error detection, because their address standard lacked a checksum. Although EIP 55 introduced such a checksum in 2016, not all wallets enforced it. Even in late 2017, people lost coins due to typos: https://bitcointalk.or g/index.php?topic=2161699.0

Enter Bech32m

To fix this bug, a new standard called bech32m was proposed.[16] It's actually a very simple change. It adds one extra number to the bech32 checksum math, which then makes sure no extra characters can be added without causing an invalid checksum.

The new standard is only used for Taproot and future addresses. For SegWit, nothing changes, because it's already protected by the 20- or 32-byte length constraint. At the time of writing, most wallet software supports the new bech32m standard.

How I Learned to Stop Worrying and Love Quantum

As an aside, Pay-to-Public-Key-Hash (P2PKH) was thought to be safer against quantum attacks, because you didn't have to say which public key you had. The downside was that the hash consumed more block space — but this wasn't an issue back then, because blocks were nowhere near full.

Many people are worried that quantum computers will eventually break the security offered by Bitcoin's cryptography, allowing future quantum hackers to steal coins, potentially crashing the market if they steal millions.

The problem is that, despite widespread P2PKH use, there's 5 to 10 million BTC out there for which the public key is already known. The irony is that because so much BTC is already vulnerable to quantum theft, there's no use trying to protect the rest. Even if your coins won't be stolen, they'll be worthless from the price crash.

The (un)likeliness of such quantum troubles in the near future, as well as possible countermeasures, is explained in

---

[16]Bech32m spec (BIP 350) https://en.bitcoin.it/wiki/BIP_0350

two *What Bitcoin Did* podcast episodes — with physicist Stepan Snigirev[17] and mathematician Andrew Poelstra.[18]

Block space is much scarcer now, so not having to put public key hashes on precious block space would save users fees. This is why in the new Taproot soft fork (see part V), Bitcoin addresses are P2PK again.[19,20] Note that the use of Taproot addresses isn't mandatory, so if you don't agree with the above reasoning, you can simply choose to not use Taproot.

---

[17]https://www.whatbitcoindid.com/podcast/the-quantum-threat-to-bitcoin-with-quantum-physicist-dr-stepan-snigirev

[18]https://www.whatbitcoindid.com/podcast/andrew-poelstra-on-schnorr-taproot-graft-root-coming-to-bitcoin

[19]Full rationale in BIP 341: https://github.com/bitcoin/bips/blob/master/bip-0341.mediawiki#cite_note-2

[20]https://twitter.com/pwuille/status/1409560741489778688

Chapter 2

DNS Bootstrap and Tor V3

Ep. 13

Bitcoin Core 0.21 added support for Tor V3 addresses in 2020.[1] This chapter will explain what this means and why it matters. It'll also discuss how new Bitcoin nodes find existing Bitcoin nodes when they bootstrap to the network.

How Does Tor Work?

When you see a Tor address,[2] it looks quite weird. That's because it's not a human readable name like a domain, but rather a public key that refers to a hidden service somewhere on the internet. The way you communicate to that hidden service isn't directly — because you don't know its IP address — but rather indirectly, through the Tor network.

---

[1]https://github.com/bitcoin/bitcoin/pull/19954

[2]e.g. https://bitcoincore.org can also be reached using a Tor browser at http://6hasakffvppilxgehrswmffqurlcjjjhd76jgvaqmsg6ul25s7t3rzyd.onion/

Tor (short for The Onion Router) is an onion network, in which messages are passed around the network through multiple hops (or servers), with each hop peeling off one encrypted layer, like an onion. The last hop sends a message to the final destination, which peels off the final encryption layer that reveals the actual message. This makes it easy to maintain anonymity and security.

To connect, you use the Tor browser.[3] This browser constructs onion packages for you. The messages are just the usual things browsers communicate: asking for an HTML document or image, and, in the other direction, receiving said document or image. The Tor browser first creates a message, which goes on the inside.[4] It wraps another message around it — which only the last hop before the hidden service can read — with instructions about where the final destination is. It then wraps another message with instructions for the second-to-last hop on how to reach the last hop, and so forth and so on.

Under the hood, this process uses IP addresses, but you don't know the IP address of the destination Tor node you're communicating with. Instead, you're communicating with other Tor nodes, and each of those nodes communicates with its direct peers. So, everyone only knows the IP addresses of their direct peers, but they don't know where a message originated from or where it ends up. Additionally, they can't read the message because it's encrypted.

To support this, all of these Tor nodes have their own sort of IP address — their onion address — and that's what you're communicating with directly. Meanwhile, Bitcoin Core nodes can run behind such a hidden service, which means everybody can have their Bitcoin node run at a secret location, resulting in IP addresses remaining secret.

---

[3]https://www.torproject.org/download/ ▨

[4]It's slightly more complicated: To protect the privacy of the recipient, the sender only wraps onions up until a rendezvous hop, which then forwards the message.

Running a Bitcoin Node behind Tor

For various reasons you might not want the rest of the world to know that your IP address is running a Bitcoin node. In particular, you may not want your Bitcoin addresses associated with your IP address, since the former says how much money you have, and the latter can often be tied directly to your name and address — not just by governments, but also by someone with access to e.g. a hacked e-commerce database with the IP addresses and home addresses of its customers. This can lead to bad outcomes.[5]

Bitcoin nodes already try to behave in ways that make them look indistinguishable from other nodes. Ideally, a node doesn't reveal to other nodes which coins it controls. A node downloads the entire blockchain and keeps track of all transactions in the mempool,[6] as opposed to only fetching the information about its own coins.

Unfortunately the system isn't perfect. Especially when you're sending and receiving transactions from your IP address, careful network analysis by an adversary can sometimes reveal where those transactions originated. This type of analysis is a billion-dollar business, where companies don't always behave ethically.[7]

Therefore, using Bitcoin from behind Tor[8] may improve your privacy by severing the link between your IP address and any information about you that your node may accidentally reveal.

---

[5]https://github.com/jlopp/physical-bitcoin-attacks

[6]The mempool is a queue of transactions that have not yet been confirmed in a block. For a *Bitcoin, Explained* episode about the mempool, see appendix A. When the mempool contains many transactions, fees tend to go up. See e.g. https://mempool.space/

[7]https://www.coindesk.com/business/2021/09/21/leaked-slides-show-how-chainalysis-flags-crypto-suspects-for-cops/, https://www.coindesk.com/markets/2019/03/05/coinbase-pushes-out-ex-hacking-team-employees-following-uproar/

[8]https://github.com/bitcoin/bitcoin/blob/master/doc/tor.md

As a practical matter, if you were already doing this, there's a new type of onion address as a result of an update in the Tor protocol: Tor V3. These new Tor addresses are longer, which makes them more secure.[9] However, this increased length required an upgrade to Bitcoin Core to support.

Bitcoin Nodes and Gossip

Why did the longer Tor V3 address require a Bitcoin Core upgrade? This has to do with how Bitcoin nodes spread the word about where they are. Nodes communicate with each other in a gossip network: They send each other lists of known nodes, and they ask each other, "Hey, which Bitcoin nodes do you know?" In return, they get a list of IP addresses, which are usually IPv4 or IPv6 addresses.

IPv6 addresses were formalized in 1998 with the intention of replacing IPv4, because the number of IPv4 addresses was limited. There are nearly 4.3 billion potential unique IPv4 addresses,[10] whereas there are enough IPv6 addresses for every molecule in the universe.

Bitcoin nodes keep lists of other Bitcoin nodes and their IP addresses, both IPv4 and IPv6. Now the way they communicate a Tor address is to piggyback on IPv6. If an "address" starts with fd87::d87e::eb43, then Bitcoin Core knows that what follows should be interpreted as a Tor address. RFC-4193 ensures that such addresses won't clash with any computer in the real world.[11]

The problem with Tor V3 addresses is they're 32 bytes, which is twice as long as an IPv6 address. That doesn't fit in the RFC-4193 piggyback mechanism, so nodes had no way to communicate those addresses.

---

[9]https://blog.torproject.org/v3-onion-services-usage
[10]https://en.wikipedia.org/wiki/IPv4
[11]https://datatracker.ietf.org/doc/html/rfc4193

Fortunately in 2019, Wladimir van der Laan wrote a new standard — BIP155 — for how to communicate addresses.[12] It introduces the new ADDRv2 message, which nodes can use to gossip those new Tor addresses (among other things). A major improvement is that each message specifies the type of address along with the address itself. This removes the need to piggyback. There are various address types, including the new Tor one, and each address type can have a different length. So, in the future, if a new address format comes along, it's not going to be a problem.[13]

The nice thing about this new peer-to-peer message is that old nodes just ignore it. And if your node knows it's talking to an old node, it won't use ADDRv2. So newer nodes will know this new message and can communicate all these new address types, and old the nodes carry on like nothing happened. Unless you want to use Tor V3, you're not required to upgrade.

However, since the Tor project *is* centralized, it can and did force users to — with a long grace period — upgrade from Tor V2 to V3. So if you relied on Tor V2 for the privacy of your Bitcoin node, you'll have no choice but to upgrade your node.

How DNS Works

But how do you connect to that first node or bootstrap to the network?[14]

Assume you just downloaded Bitcoin Core or some other client, and you started up. Now what? Is it just going to

---

[12]https://github.com/bitcoin/bips/blob/master/bip-0155.mediawi ki#Specification 🔲

[13]For example, I2P (Invisible Internet Project, an alternative to Tor) support was added in 2021: https://github.com/bitcoin/bitcoin/blob/ 7740ebcb023089d03cd2373da16305a4e501cfad/doc/i2p.md 🔲

[14]https://stackoverflow.com/questions/41673073/how-does-the-bitcoin-client-determine-the-first-ip-address-to-connect 🔲

guess random IP addresses? No. It needs to know at least one other node to connect to, but preferably more than that. The way it tries to connect is using something called DNS seeds. The internet DNS system is used for websites, e.g. you type an address like www.google.com, and what your browser does is it asks a DNS server what IP addresses are from that Google domain.

The DNS system is ultimately centralized. So basically, if you run a website, your hosting provider will have a DNS server that points to your website, and your country will have a DNS server that points to your hosting provider, and your internet provider will have a DNS server that points to all these different countries, etc.

If you're maintaining a website, you usually have to go into a control panel and type in the IP address of your server, as well as your domain name, and that's stored on the DNS server. One of the fields you have to fill out is the timeout. This is how long others on the internet may assume this IP address still belongs to your website.

So, when you're visiting a website, you're going to ask your ISP, "Hey, do you know the IP address for this website?" If it doesn't, it's going to ask the next DNS server up the street, "Do you know it?" And then as soon as it finds a record, it's going to say, "OK, is this record still valid or is this expired?" If it's still valid, it'll use it, and if it's expired, it'll go up closer and closer to the actual hosting provider. So it's basically cached.

Because of this caching, DNS records are stored very redundantly. That's good for both privacy and availability.

Bitcoin kind of abuses this system, because Bitcoin nodes aren't websites. There are a couple of Core developers who run DNS seeds, which are essentially DNS servers. And we're just pretending that, for example, seed.bitcoin.sprovoost.nl is a "website," and when you ask that "website" what its IP address is, you get a whole list of IP addresses. However, those IP addresses are Bitcoin nodes, and every time you ask, it's going to give you different IP addresses.

A DNS seed is just a simple crawler.[15] It calls a random Bitcoin node, asks it for all the nodes it knows, keeps a list, goes through the list, and pings them all. Then, once it's done pinging them all, it's just going to ping them all again.

This means that the standard infrastructure of the internet — including all the ISPs in the world — is caching a huge list of Bitcoin nodes that you can connect to, because it thinks they're just websites. It also allows Bitcoin to piggyback on any protections against censorship built into DNS.[16]

So We Trust These Developers?

What if one of the DNS seed operators were to lie and provide a list of fake or somehow malicious nodes? Perhaps as part of an elaborate eclipse attack (see chapter 7). Nothing would stop them, but it would be very visible. Anyone can request IP addresses from the DNS seed and then check if they actually load to Bitcoin nodes or not, and if these nodes are behaving in suspicious ways. This visibility discourages cheating.

Another potential problem would be if none of the DNS seeds are reachable because, for example, they're offline. For that scenario inside the Bitcoin Core source code (and thus also the binary you download) is a list of IP addresses, as well as some hidden services.

Every six months or so, all the DNS seed maintainers are asked to provide a list of the most reliable nodes — just all the nodes sorted by how frequently they're online, i.e. which DNS seeds keep track of. The Bitcoin Core developers

---

[15]https://github.com/sipa/bitcoin-seeder

[16]Matt Corallo tried to take things even further by publishing block headers via DNS: https://github.com/bitcoin/bitcoin/pull/16834

combine that information from all the DNS seed operators and that goes into the source code.[17]

Both DNS seeds and the baked-in fallback addresses are, ideally, only used once in the lifetime of your node: when it starts up for the very first time. After that, your node keeps track of the nodes it learns about by storing all these gossiped nodes in a file. When it restarts, it opens the file and tries some random nodes from it. Only if it runs out of new IP address to try, or if it takes too long, does it ask the seeds again.

Whenever a node connects to you for the first time, one of the first things it asks is: "Who else do you know?" Your node can even send IP addresses to its peers unsolicited. In particular, it announces its own IP address to them. As your IP addresses is gossiped further around the network, you start getting inbound connections.

And with that, your node is up and running!

---

[17]https://github.com/bitcoin/bitcoin/blob/v22.0/contrib/seeds/ nodes_main.txt

Chapter 3

SegWit

Ep. 32

Segregated Witness, also known as SegWit, was a soft fork activated on the Bitcoin network in the summer of 2017. It was the last soft fork before Taproot activated in the fall of 2021, and it's arguably still the biggest Bitcoin protocol upgrade to date.

In short, SegWit allowed transaction data and signature data to be separated within Bitcoin blocks. This chapter will explain how it works and go into detail about the benefits of it.

Why Segregate Witnesses?

Before SegWit arrived on the scene, there was a problem with transaction malleability. Each transaction has a unique identifier. When someone sends you coins and you send them onward to someone else, your transaction (B) uses the identifier (ID) of transaction (A) to refer to it. Now if both transactions are unconfirmed, a problem can arise when a malicious person grabs transaction A and manipulates it. This manipulation changes A's ID. As a result, transaction B now uses an outdated identifier to refer to transaction A, which means it refers to a void. A transaction that tries to spend from a void is invalid and never makes it into a block. This is a confusing experience in the best case.

A well-known example of transaction malleability, is what happened with Mt. Gox, a bitcoin exchange from Japan.[1] According to some sources, Mt. Gox was doing its internal accounting based on transaction IDs. A customer would withdraw funds, use malleability to change the withdrawal transaction a little bit and receive the money because the transaction was still valid, but then claim, "I made a withdrawal but never received the money." In response, Mt. Gox would use the transaction ID and look to see if it was in the blockchain. It'd see there wasn't a transaction ID in the blockchain that matched, reason the customer was right, and resend the coins.[2]

More specifically, the part of the transaction being manipulated is the signature: Every transaction is signed with a cryptographic signature. Prior to SegWit, there were lots of ways to tweak this signature so that it looks different but is still valid, with the amount and recipient unchanged. Only the transaction ID changes.

One way was to put a minus in front of the signature — remember a signature is just a big number — and anybody could do that.[3] When you broadcast a transaction, it goes from your node to another, and onwards from there. The aforementioned malicious person would see that transaction appear on their node, grab it, flip this bit and send it onward. At that point two versions of the same transaction are being spread through the network, and only one of them will make it into the next block.

---

[1]For a deep dive into the demise of Mt. Gox, listen to https://www.whatbitcoindid.com/mtgox-interviews

[2]https://en.wikipedia.org/wiki/Mt._Gox#Withdrawals_halted;_trading_suspended;_bitcoin_missing_(2014)

[3]Resolved with BIP 66: https://en.bitcoin.it/wiki/BIP_0066

So you may ask yourself, "Why is this a problem?" It's not necessarily a problem in the scenario we started with, where you receive coins and send them onwards. If a malleated version of transaction A makes it into the block, you just make a new transaction (B) that refers to A's new transaction ID.

But imagine you sent a transaction (A) to a super secure vault in the Arctic located thousands of meters underground. And then you went to the Arctic and created a redeem transaction (B) back to your hot wallet, and you signed it, but you didn't yet broadcast it. Then, once you broadcast the first transaction (A) to send some money to the vault and somebody messes with it, suddenly the second transaction (B) is no longer valid, since it refers to the unaltered one (A). Now you have to go back to the Arctic to create a new transaction (B) that refers to the altered version (A) — a scenario that's complicated at best.[4]

Another, perhaps more down to earth, example of how this becomes a problem is with the Lightning network,[5] which is where you're building unconfirmed transactions on top of each other. So if one of the underlying transactions is tweaked, the transactions that follow up on that one are no longer valid.

In the Lightning protocol two people send money to a shared address, and the only way to get money out of that address is by using a special transaction that both parties signed *before* they sent money into the shared address. You don't want somebody messing with the transaction that goes into the address, because then you can't spend from it anymore — or rather, you can, but you both have to sign it again. That potentially gives one party the power to blackmail the other to get their fair share of the coins back.

---

[4]This example may seem contrived, but vault designs have to take malleability into account. https://bitcoinops.org/en/topics/vaults/ ▒

[5]The book doesn't cover Lightning, but see appendix A.

Solving Transaction Malleability

So it's easy to see how much of an issue this was.

A transaction consists of all the transaction data and the signature. It's identified by the transaction ID, which, before SegWit, was the hash of those two things. For example, the 10 BTC transaction from Satoshi to Hal Finney is f4184fc5...[6]

However, because the signature can be tweaked, the hash (transaction ID) can also be tweaked, and you end up with basically the same transaction but with a different transaction ID. That's the problem that needed to be solved: somehow either making sure the signature can't be modified, or that such a modification won't change the transaction hash. The first approach appears to be very difficult if not impossible,[7] so SegWit involves the second approach.

The solution was to append the signature to the end of a transaction. This new transaction part isn't included when calculating the identifier hash. It's also not given to old nodes. As far as old nodes are concerned, the signature is empty and anyone can spend the transaction.[8] Because the new signature part isn't included in the transaction hash, its identifier doesn't change when the signature changes. Both new nodes, which have the signature, and old nodes which don't, can calculate the transaction ID and it's identical for both.

---

[6]f4184fc596403b9d638783cf57adfe4c75c605f6356fbc91338530e9831e9e16 https://bitcointalk.org/index.php?topic=155054.0 ▦

[7]https://en.bitcoin.it/wiki/BIP_0062 ▦>

[8]To be more precise: The `scriptSig` is empty, where before it would've put a public key and signature on the stack. In turn, the `scriptPubKey` is a 0 followed by a public key hash. To old nodes, this combination results in a non-zero item on the stack, i.e. `True`, which is a valid spend. On the other hand, SegWit-enabled nodes will interpret the `scriptPubKey` as a SegWit v0 program and use the new `witness` field when evaluating. See https://en.bitcoin.it/wiki/BIP_0141 ▦

In short, SegWit solved the transaction malleability issue, where transaction IDs could be altered without invalidating the transactions themselves. In turn, solving the transaction malleability issue enabled second-layer protocols like the Lightning network.

SegWit as a Soft Fork

How could SegWit be deployed as a soft fork (backward-compatible upgrade)? We'll dive more deeply into how soft forks work in chapter 12, but the basic idea is that upgraded nodes are aware of the new rules, while un-upgraded nodes don't perceive a violation of the rules.

With SegWit this is achieved by appending data to the end of a block, kind of like a subblock, and not sending that data to legacy nodes. A hash of this data is added to the coinbase transaction[9] in an `OP_RETURN` statement.

An `OP_RETURN` typically signifies that transaction verification is done, but it can be followed by text, which is then ignored. So old nodes just see an `OP_RETURN` statement, they don't care what follows, and they won't ask for the additional data. New nodes make an exception to this rule when it comes to the coinbase transaction, they do check the hash. A SegWit node verifies that the witness data is correct by comparing it to this hash. It also expects this extra data to be present, and will request it from other SegWit aware nodes if necessary.

Block Size Limit

Before SegWit, blocks had a one-megabyte limit, and that limit included the transaction data, plus all the signatures,

---

[9]The company Coinbase was named after this first transaction in a block, which creates coins out of nowhere and pays the miner their reward.

plus a little bit of block header data. Today, because SegWit transactions put their signature data in a separate place that old nodes won't see, blocks can be larger. Theoretically, they can be up to four megabytes, but in practice with typical transactions, it's closer to two and a half.

Because the signature (witness) data is in a place that old nodes don't see, we can bypass the one-megabyte block size limit without a hard fork. Old nodes will keep seeing a block with no more than one megabyte in it, but new nodes are aware of the witness data, which takes the total size well over one megabyte.

However the increase isn't unlimited. SegWit nodes use a new way of calculating how data is counted, which gives a 75 percent discount to this segregated signature data. The percentage is somewhat arbitrary — enough to make SegWit transactions cheaper than their pre-SegWit counterparts, but not so much to incentivize abuse.

Future SegWit Versions, e.g. Taproot

The topic of Taproot is covered in depth in chapter 11. But what's important to know here is SegWit's script versioning allows for easier upgrades to new transaction types, and the recent Taproot upgrade is the first example of this feature.

The versioning works as follows, and is also touched on in chapter 1, which covers addresses. The output of each transaction contains the amount and something called the scriptPubKey. The latter is a piece of Bitcoin script that constrains how to spend this coin, as we briefly mentioned in chapter 1 and will explain in more detail in chapter 10. With SegWit, the scriptPubKey always starts with a number, which is interpreted as the SegWit version. The rules for interpreting SegWit version 0 are set in stone, as are those for interpreting SegWit version 1, aka Taproot. But anything following a 2 or higher is up for grabs: Those rules may be written later.

Before a new soft fork activates, anything following an unknown version number is ignored, thus it's anyone-can-spend. As we'll explain in chapter 12 one of the things that could go wrong with soft fork activation is that a majority of miners aren't actually enforcing the new rules. But as long as most miners do enforce the new rules, they'll ensure that these anyone-can-spend outputs, from the perspective of old nodes, won't actually get spent.

Miners that run updated node software consider blocks that spend these coins invalid. And as long as they're in the majority, they'll also create the longest chain. So now the new nodes are happy because all the new rules are being followed, and the old nodes are happy because no rules are being broken from their perspective and they just follow the longest chain. So the network stays in consensus.

Hardware Wallets

In addition to all the aforementioned benefits — fixing malleability, increasing block size, versioning, etc. — SegWit introduces a commitment to the inputs, which primarily benefits hardware wallets.

A hardware wallet is an external device that holds your private keys and can sign Bitcoin transactions. Because the device is purpose built and otherwise very simple, it's less likely than your regular computer to have malware on it. It usually shows you a summary, based on its understanding of a transaction, and then asks you to approve the transaction before it actually signs.

Before signing a transaction, the device shows you the destination address and amount. That way you can verify that an attacker didn't swap out the address for one they control.

The device also checks that the input amounts add up to the output plus the fee. This protects you against a scenario where an attacker makes you pay an absurd amount of fees (perhaps colluding with a miner).

However, transactions don't actually specify their input amounts. The only way for the device to learn those is if you give it the input transactions. It can then inspect their output amounts. But having to send all the input transactions to the hardware wallet can be problematic, especially when they're big, because these devices tend to be slow and have very limited memory resources.

To be clear, any wallet should perform these checks — not just hardware wallets. You always have inputs, which are coins you own. And then you have the outputs, which are coins you're sending, including a change output to yourself usually. The difference between them is the fee the miner keeps, and the fee isn't mentioned in the transaction, so the wallet calculates it for you.

This works for a regular wallet, because it knows how much all of the inputs are worth. But a hardware wallet is disconnected from the internet, so it doesn't necessarily know how much all the inputs are worth. Without that information, it can't be sure how much money it's about to send.

Therefore, a hardware wallet has the risk that it's sending 10 million coins as a fee without realizing it. And if somebody colludes with the miner or just wants to take your coins hostage in some weird way, that's not good. So what SegWit does is it commits to those inputs.[10]

What SegWit adds to this is that, before creating a signature, the output amount is added to the data that's signed. The device now receives these amounts, along with the transaction it needs to sign. It uses that to inform the

---

[10]Unfortunately, the approach used by SegWit still left some potential attacks open, but these have been addressed by Taproot.

user and to create the signature. If your computer lied to
the device about the amount, then the resulting signature is
invalid. So the device no longer needs to look at the actual
previous transaction.

Note that nothing is stopping your computer from craft-
ing a fake transaction with fake inputs and any output
amount it wants — the hardware wallet will happily sign it.
But when your computer then broadcasts it to the network
to get it included in the blockchain, it's just not going to be
valid. So it's pointless for an attacker to try this.

Recap

The main benefit of SegWit is that it fixes malleability,
which enables things like the Lightning network, resulting
in a pretty big increase in potential transaction throughput.

The second benefit is an increase in block size, even
though this is dwarfed by the capacity increase Lightning
could achieve. The third is versioning, which makes it easier
to deploy future upgrades. And the fourth is improved
hardware wallet support.

Block Size War

If the above sounds great and uncontroversial, it's because,
in my opinion, it is. There was, however, a lot of drama in
the years surrounding this soft fork. One account of this is
provided in Jonathan Bier's *The Blocksize War: The battle
over who controls Bitcoin's protocol rules.*[11]

---

[11]https://www.amazon.com/Blocksize-War-controls-Bitcoins-
protocol/dp/B08YQMC2WM

Chapter 4

libsecp256k1 (Software Libraries)

Ep. 09

libsecp256k1[1] is a library that some people might have heard about in passing, but many don't really understand it in depth, nor do they grasp its importance. This chapter will discuss what it is and why it matters for Bitcoin. But before tackling that, an overview of libraries in general would be helpful.

A library is a reusable piece of software. According to Techopedia,[2] "A software library is a suite of data and programming code that is used to develop software programs and applications." An example of this in the cryptography world is OpenSSL: It's a piece of software that lets you perform a variety of cryptographic operations — from creating random numbers, to signing stuff with every curve under the sun. A library isn't an actual program itself, in that it doesn't do anything independently. However, other programs can use a library like OpenSSL — or a subset of it

---

[1]https://github.com/bitcoin-core/secp256k1
[2]https://www.techopedia.com/definition/3828/software-library

— to accomplish desired actions without having to write all the code themselves.

In the case of OpenSSL, users download Bitcoin Core, which is the most popular software used to connect to the Bitcoin network. Its binary file contains Bitcoin Core-specific items, along with a lot of relevant libraries. One of those libraries is OpenSSL. Or rather, *was*, as we'll explain later.

From the beginning, OpenSSL was in Bitcoin for everything cryptography related, such as signing transactions and generating secure random private keys. Satoshi had to pick one of the cryptographic curves offered by the library. For various reasons about which we can only speculate,[3] he picked the secp256k1 curve. As a result, he didn't have to write the necessary cryptographic functionality himself — which you never want to do yourself, because it's dangerous.[4] Additionally, Satoshi didn't pick the superior Schnorr signature scheme, a topic that will be covered in chapter 11, because OpenSSL didn't support it and there was no other library for it either.

With every Bitcoin Core release, the necessary library is included in the file you can download. Not all software includes all its libraries. The alternative is to make use of libraries that are already present on your computer, which makes the download smaller, as the library doesn't have to be redownloaded. However, this can create problems.

The most obvious problem of not including all libraries in the download is that the user may not have one or more of the required libraries. They'd then have to be instructed to download them, which is a bad user experience. As an aside, this is actually a common experience in the life of software developers, who spend much of their time chasing

---

[3]See the "Choosing The Right Elliptic Curve" section in this article by (pre-Ethereum) Vitalik Buterin: https://bitcoinmagazine.com/te chnical/satoshis-genius-unexpected-ways-in-which-bitcoin-dodged-some-cryptographic-bullet-1382996984

[4]https://security.stackexchange.com/a/18198/209204

down libraries and other dependencies for the professional tools they try to install. The experience is often recursive, where each library in turn depends on yet another library.

Another concern is that libraries can and do change. The library on your system may be too old or too new. Critical things may have changed that cause the library to no longer be compatible with the program that relies on it.[5] The last thing you want when dealing with cryptographic stuff is to be surprised about what's on your computer.

Including libraries in the download means you always have the right version. This is why your computer probably contains many copies and versions of the same libraries.

But even when libraries are included in a download, things can go wrong when a software developer decides to update a library to a newer version.

Someone out there is maintaining the library. They don't have time to test each of their changes in every single software package out there that uses their library. So if you're not paying attention to what the library maintainer is doing — either by looking at changes in the release notes or by checking out the code itself — they might break something.

Then, when you download the library along with the rest of Bitcoin Core, your computer now uses that changed part of the library. But what if the Bitcoin Core developers didn't notice this particular change that happened to the library? Then, all of a sudden, the stuff they wanted Bitcoin Core to do isn't actually happening.

Most breaking changes in libraries are accidents, but not all. Chapter 9 goes deeper into the process of checking dependencies and attacks from rogue dependency maintainers.

A breaking change in how a library behaves is particularly problematic when it causes a change in the interpretation of

---

[5]The changes in libraries over time make it difficult to compile and run old versions of Bitcoin Core, even though the source code is still available. This will be a problem for future archeologists. https://blog.lopp.net/running-bitcoin-core-v0-7-and-earlier/

the rules of the blockchain: Bitcoin Core would consider a particular block valid in one version of the library, and in another version, it'd consider that same block invalid. This leads to a chain split.[6]

This is exactly what happened with a past version of Bitcoin Core: There was a bug in OpenSSL, which meant the developers of Bitcoin Core had to upgrade OpenSSL because the old version was simply no longer safe. But unbeknownst to the Core developers, there was another change in OpenSSL when they upgraded.

This particular change dealt with what happened with signatures and whether or not they're considered valid. The original version of OpenSSL was pretty relaxed, so it would accept signatures as valid even if they didn't meet the exact specifications. They couldn't be signed by somebody else, so it wasn't about stealing funds, but it was more about the fact that the notation could be a bit sloppy.

Now, the new version was extremely picky. If you used Bitcoin software to create a transaction, that wasn't a problem, because any Bitcoin transaction was signed strictly, according to the protocol. And if you decided to validate these transactions using old software, it would see the sloppy version that was also made with the old software, and it wouldn't have an issue with the transaction. However, the new software would say it's invalid, because it doesn't accept these sloppy signatures. So all of a sudden, there's an accidental soft fork, which is what happens when previously valid transactions become invalid.

Fortunately, some developers became aware of this problem in time. Had they not noticed this, there could've been a big chain split once the updated OpenSSL library was bundled in a Bitcoin Core release binary. Instead, several measures were taken to defuse this timebomb.

---

[6]https://coinmarketcap.com/alexandria/glossary/chain-split

First, users could still download the Bitcoin Core binary as usual, since it came bundled with this older version of OpenSSL. Even though this version had a security bug in it, remember that each piece of software on your computer can choose to bring its own version of OpenSSL. This particular bug[7] impacted browser software, but not Bitcoin Core, so your browser would have to ship the new version immediately, while Bitcoin Core could wait a little longer.

Second, those who prefer to compile their own software from source were offered two possible workarounds.[8] They could either hold off on updating OpenSSL, or use a sufficiently recent version of the source code, which now contained a patch that worked around the issue.

Third, the BIP 66 soft fork was proposed,[9] and it was indeed successfully activated (read more on soft fork activation in chapter 12). This fork required that future signatures all abide by the stricter standard, so that both old and new versions of OpenSSL would accept them.

This incident wasn't necessarily surprising, as OpenSSL is famous for its vulnerabilities. The main reason for this is because these libraries have been used by everyone for decades, but they're only maintained by a tiny number of volunteers on a shoestring budget.

cURL[10] is another example of this. It's a library that downloads files, and it's used everywhere, but again, there isn't a well-funded team behind it.

In the case of OpenSSL, one reason it had these bugs is that it's easy to make mistakes with cryptographic code. What's more, OpenSSL is written in C, so if you forget a semicolon, whoops, now you're skipping a line, and perhaps

---

[7]https://nvd.nist.gov/vuln/detail/CVE-2014-8275

[8]https://lists.linuxfoundation.org/pipermail/bitcoin-dev/2015-January/007097.html

[9]https://en.bitcoin.it/wiki/BIP_0066

[10]https://github.com/curl/curl

that line was actually checking the password. A famous example of this is the Heartbleed[11] bug from 2014, in which a small mistake made it so anyone with the know-how could log into any computer on the internet without a password.

When a bug in Bitcoin isn't discovered and fixed in time, a malicious person can trigger a sudden network split. In the example above, someone could've broadcast a transaction with a signature that's valid according to old versions of OpenSSL, yet invalid according to new versions of OpenSSL. This would cause old nodes to accept the block and new nodes to reject it. Chain splits can be triggered by all sorts of programming mistakes, not just changes in libraries. There have been a few close calls.[12]

While all this was happening, Pieter Wuille[13] was working on a library that was specifically designed to create and verify Bitcoin signatures. His original motivation had nothing to do with security; he just wanted it to work faster than OpenSSL.

He explains this in a podcast he did with Chaincode.[14] Basically, he wanted to make a library that would be about four times faster. He could've tried to modify the OpenSSL code itself, but it's such a nightmare to change that code. Additionally, the OpenSSL code is very generic: It has to support all different kinds of cryptography. So if you want to change anything, you have to be very abstract in all the things you do.

Instead, he decided to essentially write it from scratch, specifically for the secp256k1 curve. It was added to Bitcoin Core relatively early — first just to verify signatures, and then later on to create signatures as well.

This happened to coincide with the aforementioned secu-

---

[11]https://gizmodo.com/how-heartbleed-works-the-code-behind-the-internets-se-1561341209
[12]https://blog.bitmex.com/bitcoins-consensus-forks/
[13]https://github.com/sipa
[14]https://podcastaddict.com/episode/94276066

rity vulnerability, and the general reaction was that because there was a near miss which could've been a serious problem, moving away from OpenSSL for critical matters would be a good idea.

With signing and signature validation taken care of, Bitcoin still relied on OpenSSL for other things — though much less than it had in the past. But developers had already made the decision to get rid of the remaining OpenSSL uses over time by copying or rewriting the various parts of the library that Bitcoin Core needs. This process was completed[15] in 2019. The first version of Bitcoin Core to ship without OpenSSL was 0.20.0, which was released in June 2020.

So Wuille's libsecp256k1 — initially designed to be a performance improvement — pivoted to be a new library for Bitcoin that would remove the risks that came with OpenSSL. However, this came with two risks of its own:

- Writing your own cryptographic library (this is dangerous outside of cryptocurrency, too).
- Swapping out one critical library for another, because even the slightest difference in behavior could cause a chain split.

However, it was deemed a risk worth taking, because the other option was waiting for OpenSSL to explode. Additionally, a lot of good cryptographers reviewed libsecp256k1 and compared it against OpenSSL before its adoption. It's also used by Ethereum and other cryptocurrencies — basically, any cryptocurrency that uses the secp256k1 elliptic curve.[16]

---

[15]https://github.com/bitcoin/bitcoin/pull/17265 ▓

[16]https://en.bitcoin.it/wiki/Secp256k1 ▓

Part II

Resource Usage

Overview

The blockchain is big. Resources like CPU power, RAM and internet bandwidth are increasing every year, thanks to Moore's law, but they are still scarce and not equally distributed in the world. They're also not guaranteed to go on forever.

Despite a limit on block size, improvements in hardware and many improvements to Bitcoin software, the cost of running a full node is expected to keep *increasing* over the next few decades. Contrary to what you might expect from the fierce debates about block size, disk space is actually the least of the problems.

What can we do about that?

Chapter 5

Sync Time and AssumeUTXO

Ep. 14

One of the biggest bottlenecks — if not the biggest one — for scaling Bitcoin is initial block download. This is the time it takes for a Bitcoin node to synchronize with the Bitcoin network, as it needs to process all historic transactions and blocks to construct the latest unspent transaction output (UTXO) set, i.e. the current state of Bitcoin ownership.

This chapter will cover some of the ways sync time has been sped up over time. It was first improved through Headers First synchronization, which ensures that new Bitcoin nodes don't waste time validating (potentially) weaker blockchains. One of several recent improvements to synchronizing time is called Assume Valid, a default shortcut that lets nodes skip signature verification of older transactions, instead trusting that the Bitcoin Core development process — in combination with the resource-expensive nature of mining — offers a reliable version of transaction history.

It'll also discuss how the security assumptions underpinning Assume Valid could be extended to allow for a potential future upgrade, AssumeUTXO, to offer new Bitcoin Core users a speedy solution to get up to speed with the Bitcoin network by syncing the most recent blocks first and checking historical blocks in the background later.

In addition to the accompanying *Bitcoin, Explained* episode, you can also listen to an episode of *The Chaincode Podcast* with AssumeUTXO author James O'Beirne, which covers the same topics as this chapter.[1]

Downloading the Blockchain

When you turn on your Bitcoin node it finds and connects to other peers, as we explained in chapter 2. It then proceeds to download the blockchain.

The most naive way of downloading the blockchain would be to just ask your peers to send you everything they've got. That's not a good idea, because if any of your peers are malicious, they could trick you into downloading terabytes of fake blocks, until you run out of disk space and your node crashes.

To prevent such abuse the initial version of Bitcoin would first ask nodes for a block header. This header includes the proof-of-work, which — as the term suggests — proves that some work went into creating the block. By checking the proof in this header before fetching the block itself, it makes it more expensive for an attacker to produce enough fake blocks to overflow your hard disk. Once the block is fetched and checked, your node asks for the next header, and so forth, processing headers and blocks sequentially.[2]

---

[1]https://podcast.chaincode.com/2020/02/12/james-obeirne-4.html

[2]It was slightly more complicated. When a node received a block that didn't directly build on the tip of its chain, it would, as Satoshi put it in a source code comment, "shunt it off to [a] holding area." From there, it could be appended to the chain tip later. These blocks were called *orphan blocks*, a term often mixed up with *stale blocks*.

Although this protects against the most trivial form of block spam, we're not out of the woods. The approach is still very myopic, in that your node only checks the blocks right in front of it, without seeing the big picture.

The problem with this is you don't know if you're following a dead end, and someone could feed your node a long branch of blocks that aren't part of the most proof-of-work chain. Nodes that just came online are especially vulnerable to this. This is because the proof-of-work difficulty has historically increased. It's expensive to create dead-end branches that start from recent blocks, because many miners are competing to produce blocks, pushing up the cost of creating a block. But if an attacker starts from a very old block, from a time when there were fewer and less powerful miners, then the cost to produce these blocks is very low.

So an attacker can create a chain of very low difficulty blocks that branch off from some old block. If your node is new in town, when it sees two — or even thousands of — possible branches, it doesn't know which is the real one. If it picks the branch from the attacker first, it can end up wasting lots of time and computer resources to verify the blocks. Even though the proof-of-work difficulty of these blocks is low, it's not any easier for a node to verify the transactions; these dead-end branches may be filled to their one megabyte maximum with specially crafted transactions that are verified extra slowly.

In addition to bogging down nodes with dead-end branches of low difficulty blocks, there's also the issue of eclipse attacks, which we'll cover in chapter 7.

Checkpoints

One solution to this problem was the use of checkpoints: Developers would put the hash and height of several known valid blocks in the source code, and any new block that didn't descend from one of these checkpoints would be ignored. This didn't completely undo dead-end branches, but it limited their maximum length.

The downside of checkpoints is that they potentially give a lot of power to developers. A malicious cabal of developers, or a benevolent dictator doing what's best for the community — whichever perspective you prefer — could decree that a certain block is valid. Even if an alternative branch with more proof-of-work exists, nodes wouldn't consider this branch.

Perhaps a developer loses their Bitcoin in a hack; they could then introduce a malicious checkpoint right before the hacked coins moved and move their coins to safety in the revised history. Such an attack can't happen in secret, and if it ever really happened, users might simply refuse to install new node software with the checkpoint. But prevention would be better.

The last checkpoint was added in late 2014. Checkpoints were made mostly unnecessary by various means, including the introduction of `nMinimumChainWork` in 2016.[3] This parameter states how much proof-of-work any chain of headers must demonstrate before even being considered. But for this to work, it requires nodes to be less myopic; they need to consider *where* a given trail of blocks leads before spending lots of computer power chasing it. And that's where Headers First comes in.

Headers First

Given enough time — and if it doesn't crash — your node would compare all blockchain branches and eventually pick the one with the most difficulty. But because it needs to verify every branch first, it could take a very long time to determine the correct one.

---

[3]https://github.com/bitcoin/bitcoin/pull/9053

So rather than downloading and verifying entire blocks, the new approach is to download and verify just the headers, which are much smaller. In particular, headers are the only thing you need to determine the cumulative proof-of-work difficulty in any given branch.

Once your node knows which branch has the most proof-of-work, it downloads the blocks for it and starts verifying. This step can't be skipped, because it's still possible there's an invalid block in the chain with the most proof-of-work. Should your node run into such an invalid block, it discards the branch and repeats the process for whichever branch had the second most proof-of-work.

Assume Valid

Assume Valid is a block hash that's encoded in the software. More specifically, it's a hash of a block from just before the last major release. Many Bitcoin Core developers publicly verify this hash, and anyone on GitHub can see the hash, and they can check for themselves whether or not the hash is real.

If you're a new user and you start Bitcoin Core, it'll sync all the headers and get all the blocks. And if that particular hash is in the chain, it won't verify any signatures that came before it. It'll still verify everything else, e.g. that the proof-of-work is valid and that no coins are created out of thin air. Skipping signature verification mainly saves CPU usage, and this speeds up the whole process.

The Assume Valid mechanism is different from a checkpoint, in that a node doesn't require that the hash occurs in the blockchain. If your node sees another branch of the blockchain without this hash, and if it has more proof-of-work, it'll consider that other branch first. The only difference is that it *will* verify the signatures for that other branch, so it'll take a bit longer.

What does it mean to not check signatures for blocks before the Assume Valid hash? It means that if somebody stole a coin, i.e. spent a UTXO with an invalid signature, your node wouldn't notice. But if someone created a coin out of thin air, your node would still see that.

This is where the transparency of source code becomes an important factor. *If* there ever was a theft of coins that Bitcoin Core developers wanted to cover up, they'd only be able to trick new nodes. First, the developers would have to produce a block that steals[4] coins by using an invalid signature. Such a block would be considered invalid by all existing nodes. Then, they'd take this invalid block, or a descendant, and use its hash as Assume Valid.

Anyone who already runs a node would be able to see this hash on GitHub and check it against their own node. They'd then either not see the block at all, or their node would point out that it's invalid (because of the invalid signature). Both would be reason to sound the alarm. Barring some immense social media censorship campaign, anyone about to download a new node might learn what's going on.

But the hypothetical malicious developers have another problem. No miners are building on top of their invalid block, because the miners already had their node software installed before the invalid hash was produced. Within hours of the developers publishing this hash, and long before they release any software for download, miners have already produced a longer chain that doesn't include this stealing block. So even if a user didn't notice the social media drama, their

---

[4]This hypothetical attack can't create coins out of nowhere, so the victim of this theft might also make some noise. However, many coins are thought to be permanently lost — e.g. because the owner lost their private keys — and those coins could make a good target. Since Satoshi disappeared, stealing coins that are allegedly his could make sense, but those coins are being very closely monitored by many people. Any block attempting to steal them, even if invalid, would probably get some media attention.

node would simply follow the longest chain. It'd be a bit slower because it couldn't use the Assume Valid feature, but it'd be fine.

So, what if developers colluded with miners in the theft? If a majority of miners decide to work with the developers and continue building on the invalid stealing block, then they'd be able to trick new users. But they wouldn't be able to trick existing users, which is generally the vast (economic) majority. Massive drama and probably massive economic losses for these miners would ensue, as no exchange would accept their deposit.

But what if developers, miners, *and* all existing users conspire to trick new users? Such a conspiracy seems impossible to coordinate secretly. But if you do worry the world is out to get you, rest assured that you can turn the Assume Valid feature off by starting your node with `-assumevalid=0`. Your node would then notice the invalid stealing block, you would yourself see its hash in the source code, and you could run to streets protesting the situation.

What's important to understand here is that developers can already collude against you and sneak bad things into the code — we'll talk more about that in chapter 9. Developers could also put in a backdoor that gives them access to your private keys. This actually happened with an altcoin called Lucky7Coin.[5] These backdoors could be very carefully hidden in the code in a way that only very skilled developers could detect. The Assume Valid hash, on the other hand, is very clearly visible, and it requires very little skill to verify, as explained above. This is why the Bitcoin Core developers believe that this feature is safe against abuse.

Assume Valid has been in Bitcoin Core since v0.14 (2017), and now there's a new proposal: AssumeUTXO.

---

[5]https://github.com/alerj78/lucky7coin/issues/1

AssumeUTXO

In early 2019, Chaincode Labs alumni James O'Beirne introduced a proposal[6] for AssumeUTXO that would allow users to get started more quickly. As mentioned earlier in the chapter, the UTXO set is the collection of coins that exists right now. Every time you send someone money, it creates an UTXO, and it destroys the UTXO you sent from. It's like you have a bank account that's closed down when you use it, and you get a fresh bank account for the change.

Today, the only way to reconstruct the UTXO set and find out which coins exist right now is to replay all Bitcoin transactions starting from the 2009 genesis block.[7] You take the first block and see which coins it creates and which coins it destroys. Then you take the second block and do the same. You have to start at the beginning and do it until the end, and you can only do it sequentially — all of which takes a long time.

AssumeUTXO instead uses a recent snapshot of the UTXO set and works from there, skipping hundreds of thousands of historical blocks. It starts out just like nodes today by performing a Headers First sync to determine which chain is the longest one. But once it has the headers, it can load the snapshot. This snapshot is of the UTXO set at a certain height — maybe just before the release. From there, it proceeds as normal, checking each new block to see which coins were destroyed and which were created, until finally, it reaches the most recent block (tip). So then you know your balance exactly and you can start using it.

But in the meantime, in the background, it starts at the genesis block, goes all the way to the snapshot, and verifies that the snapshot is correct. And if the snapshot isn't correct,

---

[6]https://github.com/bitcoin/bitcoin/issues/15605

[7]Due to a bug or great benevolence by Satoshi, nodes actually don't process the genesis block in this manner, so the very first 50 BTC ever created can't be spent. https://en.bitcoin.it/wiki/Genesis_block

it starts screaming (or it unceremoniously crashes with an error message).

With Assume Valid, it still did all of the UTXO set constructing and replayed all of the transactions; it just didn't check for the signatures. Now, with AssumeUTXO, it skips the transaction replaying altogether, or more accurately: It defers it. Instead, it takes the UTXO set at the snapshot block height, and then processes all subsequent blocks in order to construct the current UTXO set.

Does the Past Matter?

One question to ask is whether it's really useful to check historical blocks after loading the snapshot. Of course, if you're restoring an old wallet from a backup, you'll need to scan historical blocks for your transaction history, but let's disregard that scenario for now.

Assuming you're a new user, the first thing you want to do is receive coins. You want to be sure these coins will later be accepted by others. And you may want to make sure there's really a 21 million BTC limit. Do you need to check historical blocks to know this?

To start with the second question — checking the 21 million limit — the answer is *no*. You can calculate the total amount of Bitcoin in existence right now by adding up all the values in the UTXO set. And then you can look at the source to understand how many coins can be created in the future. There's no need to see past blocks for that.

However, to know if others will accept the coins you received, you need to know that the person who sent you the coins didn't create them out of thin air or steal them. This goes back to the question of if a malicious developer can get away with this. Let's look into how this compares to manipulating Assume Valid.

Let's say developers create some coins out of thin air and add them to the UXO set, or that they reassign existing coins to themselves. Anyone verifying the snapshot would find out, so again, code transparency mitigates some of this.

But where, in the Assume Valid example above, the developers would have to create an invalid block right away, before making a new software release, that's not necessary here. The new or stolen coins would exist in your UTXO set without ever having been in a block. So miners and existing node operators won't initially detect this, because there's no invalid block floating around.

But there's a catch: When you, as the new user, receive a coin that was created out of nowhere, it never gets confirmed in a block. The new transaction won't be mined, because miners have the correct UTXO set and recognize the transaction as invalid.

What if miners are in on it? Then the transaction would confirm and you'd have been fooled. However, every other node would reject the new block, and the attack would now be visible to everyone involved.

Developers could be very patient though. Instead of immediately trying to spend the from-thin-air coins, they could wait many years. Perhaps by that time, many miners will have reinstalled their node, along with the manipulated snapshot, and synced it. Perhaps many exchanges did so as well. And many regular users. So when they finally spend the from-thin-air coins, perhaps the block is only considered invalid by a small group of old school hardcore bitcoiners.

So as before, this attack requires much of the world to conspire against you, but as far as global conspiracies go, it may be ever so slightly less difficult to get away with.

One way to mitigate this attack is for every block to include a hash of the current UTXO snapshot. This would be a soft fork (see chapter 12). That way, every node verifies the snapshot, and it wouldn't have to be included in the software.

However, as things stand today, producing such a hash would increase the verification time for a block from a few seconds to more than a minute. So a different type of hash has been proposed.[8]

There will probably be a lot more discussion before such a soft fork is even proposed. At the time of writing, AssumeUTXO is still being developed. Nodes can already produce snapshots of their UTXO set, but the code to actually load and use a snapshot is still undergoing review.[9]

---

[8]MuHash: https://lists.linuxfoundation.org/pipermail/bitcoin-dev/2017-May/014337.html

[9]https://github.com/bitcoin/bitcoin/pull/15606

Chapter 6

Utreexo

Ep. 15

Whenever a new Bitcoin transaction is made, Bitcoin nodes use a UTXO set to determine that the coins being spent really exist (see chapter 5). This UTXO set is currently several gigabytes in size and continues to grow over time, and there's no upper limit to how big it can potentially get.

Because Bitcoin nodes perform best if the UTXO set is kept in RAM, and because RAM is a relatively scarce resource for computers, it would benefit a node's performance if the UTXO set could be stored in a more compact format. This is the promise of Utreexo.[1]

Utreexo would take all the UTXOs in existence and include them in a Merkle tree, which is a data structure consisting only of hashes. This chapter explains how the compact Utreexo structure could suffice in proving that a particular UTXO is included when a new transaction is made. It also covers the potential benefits that could surface if this solution were to be used, along with some of the potential tradeoffs.

---

[1]Pronounced U Tree X O. See also: https://bitcoinmagazine.com/ articles/bitcoins-growing-utxo-problem-and-how-utreexo-can-help-solve-it

54

The Challenge

When syncing a new Bitcoin node, one of the challenges is the amount of random-access memory (RAM) you have. In general, you don't need a lot of RAM on your computer, but if you want to sync fast, you do.

The reason this is necessary is due to the UTXO set, which is a list of all coins in existence, including the ones you own. Every time a new block comes in, for every transaction in it, you check that it spends coins that actually exist. You also remember which new coins the transaction created, so that you're aware of this when it gets spent in a later block. This information is held in a database, and if it's located on your hard disk, this checking and updating is a slow process. However, if the database is located in your RAM, it's extremely fast.

The time it take varies, but say you had a newer MacBook Pro with 32GB RAM, and you allowed the node to use half of this; it'd take maybe seven hours to sync the entire chain.[2] However, let's say you had a Raspberry Pi with only 2GB of RAM and a small hard drive. In this case, it could take several weeks.[3]

The key point here is that if you can keep more of the UTXO set in RAM, you'll sync faster. It'd be nice if the size of the UTXO set could be decreased, but that's not

---

[2]In late 2020, former Bitcoin Core maintainer Jonas Schnelli synced the chain on an Apple M1 in five hours. It would've been faster if he allocated more than 5GB of RAM (using `-dbcache`). In the meantime, the chain has grown, hence the more conservative estimate. https://twitter.com/_jonasschnelli_/status/1333303029370675201

[3]There are two bottlenecks. First, your node keeps as much as possible in RAM during sync, but once it fills up this memory, it has to write the UTXO database to disk, clear its memory, and start caching again. The second problem is that if the blockchain doesn't fit on the hard drive, then your node has to delete old blocks to make room for new ones. A side effect of this is that the coin database in RAM must be written to disk, further slowing down the sync process.

necessarily possible. Of course, if you're spending more coins than you're creating, then the number of UTXOs and the RAM usage both go down. However, there's a lot of junk in the UTXO set, because in the past, people created transactions to multisig addresses that were fake just to e.g. put pictures of Obama in the blockchain. And those are all sitting in your RAM because your node has no idea they're nonsense.

However, if we expect everybody in the world to eventually use Bitcoin and to have at least one or two UTXOs each, that would take terabytes of RAM, and Moore's Law[4] isn't going to catch up to this anytime soon. But even without the entire world using Bitcoin, it could get to the point where fewer and fewer people have enough RAM to sync it quickly, which is a problem. If fewer people run their own node, the system becomes less decentralized.

Utreexo

One way to address this issue is with Tadge Dryja's proposal, the Utreexo.[5] Dryja is a research scientist at the MIT Digital Currency Initiative.

Currently with Bitcoin, you can prune the archival block storage to save disk space. After your node downloads a block, processes it, and updates the UTXO set, it no longer has any use for the block. Your node knows exactly which coins exist in the UTXO set, which is all the information it needs to validate future transactions.

When pruning is enabled, your node holds on to the block for a few more days and then deletes it. This way, you need less than a gigabyte of storage, even though the blockchain itself is hundreds of gigabytes. The downside

---

[4]https://en.wikipedia.org/wiki/Moore%27s_law

[5]https://dci.mit.edu/utreexo , https://www.youtube.com/watch?v=6Y6n88DmkjU

is that you don't have the blocks, so you can't share them with other nodes. This is acceptable as long as enough other nodes still have the full archive.

With Utreexo, you're pruning the UTXO set. Instead of throwing away transactions (along with the blocks they're in), you throw away the list of coins that exist. The only thing you keep is a Merkle root, i.e. a hash that represents all the coins in existence. Every leaf of the Merkle tree represents a single UTXO, and the Merkle root commits to all of them. For each coin that you care about, e.g. because it's in your wallet, your node keeps a Merkle proof. When spending a coin, you need to attach this proof to your transaction so that other nodes can verify that the coin exists.

To put it another way, normally, when somebody sends you a transaction, the transaction says, "I'm spending this input, and you, the person running a node, have the responsibility to check whether that input exists in your own database." And here, you're flipping this around and telling the other node, "I have no idea which coins exist, because I don't have enough RAM to track all that. You prove to me that this coin actually existed." So the burden of proof is reversed, which begs the question of how.

Merkle Proof Tutorial

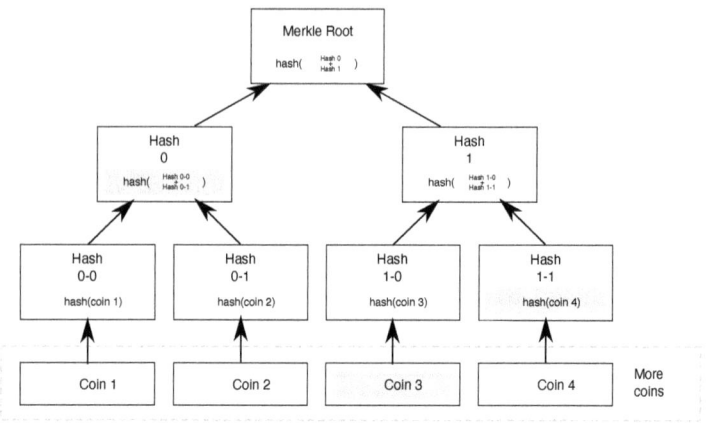

Merkle tree. To prove the existence of Coin 3, you need to provide a Merkle proof consisting of the three marked items.[6]

The figure above illustrates how you can prove the existence of Coin 3 using a Merkle proof, given a verifier that only knows the Merkle root (top). First, you reveal the coin itself, which is just a transaction output with an amount and `scriptPubKey`. The verifier hashes this to obtain Hash 1-0 (directly above Coin 3 in the figure). You then provide Hash 1-1. Even though you probably don't own Coin 4 and you may not even know its amount and `scriptPubKey`, you do know its hash, because your wallet kept track of this information. With that, the verifier can calculate Hash 1. You then provide Hash 0, and now the verifier can see that your proof results in the same Merkle root hash they knew about. You've now demonstrated ownership of Coin 3 without the need for the verifier to know the entire UTXO set.

We'll revisit Merkle trees in chapter 10 and chapter 11.

---

[6]Modified from: https://commons.wikimedia.org/wiki/File: Hash_Tree.svg

Seeing the Forest for the Trees

Currently, if someone sends a transaction to you, you check inside your node and the database with your UTXO set to see if the transaction is spending valid UTXOs. With Utreexo, the sender will have to provide you with the proof that their transaction is spending existing UTXOs. Although you no longer have to hold on to several gigabytes of UTXO data, you do still need to keep track of a few things, namely a Merkle tree — or several trees — of hashes.

All the UTXOs in existence would be put into this tree and everybody can construct this tree if they replay the whole blockchain. Basically what the tree would look like is you have the first and second UTXO next to each other. Then, you take the hash of those two — basically combined — which is one new hash. You can do that again for another two UTXOs that exist and combine their hashes. So, for example, you have four UTXOs. Two of them are shared, and then those two are shared again, and you end up with one hash.

Utreexo uses perfect trees, which means the number of leaves in each must be a power of two. Because the UTXO set contains an arbitrary number of coins, you end up with a forest of trees. For example, if there are six coins, your forest would have a tree with 2^2=4 leaves and a tree with two leaves. All your node needs to store is the Merkle root hash of each tree. There are currently a little under 100 million coins in existence.[7] Because this is less than 2^{27}, it'd take 27 trees to represent them all. Each SHA-256 hash[8] is 32 bytes, so your node needs to store 27 * 32 = 864 bytes. If every human owns multiple coins, it'd only grow to one kilobyte.

---

[7]https://txstats.com/dashboard/db/utxo-set-repartition-by-output-type ▦

[8]https://qvault.io/cryptography/how-sha-2-works-step-by-step-sha-256/ ▦

How do we update the tree for every block as leaves are removed and added, i.e. coins are spent and created? You can actually take the UTXO that's being spent out of the tree and put the new one into the tree. To do that, you need to recalculate the tree, and that's done by knowing its neighbors. We already illustrated how to prove that something exists in the tree, and it turns out that's exactly the same information you need to put something else at the bottom of the tree and then provide the root hash.

When you're syncing the blockchain, you could keep track of the entire tree, but then you'd need a lot of RAM, just like in the original scenario. This is why you only store the root of each tree. Then, when somebody has a new transaction that you want to verify, they need to give you the Merkle proofs for all the inputs they're spending to prove that they exist. They'll also tell you which outputs are there — these will be swapped in at the same places where those inputs were — and they'll tell you about any new trees being made.

Bridge Nodes

There are two ways you can learn about a transaction. Someone can send it to you via the network, in which case you add it to your mempool. Or, it can be part of a block you receive.

How would you validate the transaction in the first scenario? With Utreexo, you have the top of the trees in your RAM. The sender is responsible for sending the transaction, as well as the proof that the transaction is valid, which also includes information for you so you know where to find it in the forest. If the sender doesn't support Utreexo and doesn't provide the proof, your node could simply ignore the transaction.

But what about the second scenario? If a miner mines a block and a transaction is in there, the block doesn't contain the proof. To get this proof, you need the help of a bridge node. This is a node that has the actual UTXO set, the old-fashioned way, so it has lots of RAM or it's just slow. And it produces all these proofs and it sends them around to whoever wants them.

When a bridge node receives a transaction that doesn't have a Merkle proof, it takes the proof it has, attaches it to the transaction, and sends it to other Utreexo nodes. The same goes for entire blocks. You don't have to be directly connected to such a bridge node, as other Utreexo-aware nodes can relay blocks with the proofs attached. From the perspective of the Utreexo node, the bridge node is just a Utreexo node, and from the perspective of the old-fashioned nodes, it's just an old-fashioned node.

There's nothing magical about bridge nodes. Any node that has the original UTXO set can construct the proof for any transaction. But doing so would defeat the purpose of Utreexo, because keeping track of both the regular UTXO set and these proofs takes a lot of memory.

So these bridge nodes do the translation between the current world of nodes that track the UTXO set in memory and these new Utreexo-enabled nodes that don't have to. As long as one bridge node exists, it can bootstrap the network. However, this relies on these bridge nodes being backed by people with good intentions. But these nodes could change, or disappear, or run out of battery.

Looking at the longterm picture, if people like Utreexo given the advantages — or even if they don't like it — if the UTXO set gets too big and takes too long to sync on any normal computer, then you could basically make a soft fork that requires all proofs to be in the block.[9] By including

---

[9]You'd include the hash of the proofs somewhere in the coinbase transaction. As we explained in chapter 3 for SegWit, the proofs themselves would go in a special place inside the block that old nodes don't see.

proofs in the blocks, they're guaranteed to be available to all nodes.

The tradeoff there is that bigger blocks require more bandwidth and storage, but less RAM is used. At the moment, bandwidth is probably a bigger constraint than RAM, so a soft fork isn't likely to happen, but this could change in the decades ahead.

Cool Things

With this solution, because you wouldn't need a lot of RAM, you could start doing things in specialized hardware. For example, smartphones tend to have very little RAM, so they could get a big performance boost from Utreexo. Or, you could even have a specialized chip — like a GPU — with a tiny onboard memory that validates Bitcoin blocks.[10]

But even without specialized hardware, there's a potential speedup if the CPU can do most of the block validation work. A 1KB Merkle forest can easily be kept in a typical CPU cache.[11] This avoids having to ferry UTXO set information between the CPU and RAM. Just like using RAM to avoid physical disk reads speeds things up, so does using the CPU cache to avoid using RAM.

In chapter 5, we described how the source code contains a hash that represents the UTXO set a given snapshot height. The node still needs to obtain that UTXO set, which is several gigabytes in size, and it'd probably download it from

---

[10]Then you have the protocol literally set in stone, or at least set in silicon. If somebody wants to do a hard fork, you'd have to break all the node hardware, and not just all the mining hardware. So, that's a nice extra barrier to not do hard forks. Unfortunately, this also makes soft forks less attractive, as nodes can't verify the new rules with the accelerated hardware — so your computer would have to slow down to check all the new rules whenever it encounters transactions that fall under the new rules.

[11]https://en.wikipedia.org/wiki/CPU_cache

its peers. With Utreexo, the UTXO set is so small that it can be put in the source code, thus removing the need to download the UTXO set for the snapshot.

A Couple Tradeoffs

Although Utreexo has the potential to be cool, there are some tradeoffs. The most apparent is that if you start using it, and then later, somebody finds a better accumulator,[12] you'd have to switch. Such a switch is easy in a scenario with bridge nodes — multiple solutions could exist in parallel, each with their own bridge nodes. But once the proofs are added into blocks with a soft fork, there's no easy way back.

Another downside is that bandwidth seems to be the bottleneck for Bitcoin right now, and this could make it worse. For that reason, Utreexo is more of an option that people can opt into if, in their case, bandwidth isn't a problem. However, if the UTXO set grows to a significant degree where it does become a burden and slows down validation, then this might be more appealing.

---

[12]The general term for what Utreexo uses for its coin accounting is called an accumulator. It's something you can use to add stuff to, and in this case, to also remove stuff from. But there are all sorts of mathematical tricks you can deploy to do this. The Merkle tree is conceptually very simple, as we hopefully illustrated, but there have been other proposals, like an RSA accumulator. There's all sorts of cool cryptographic math you can do to just add things to a set and remove them from a set, essentially. It's too early to set any particular accumulator in stone with a soft fork.

Part III

Attacking Bitcoin

Overview

An important design philosophy of Bitcoin — and safety engineering in general — is to be honest about the ways in which it's potentially vulnerable. The following chapters should cause the reader to be paralyzed with fear — or at least slightly worried.

Several of the potential attacks described have never even happened in practice. Nonetheless, we want to prevent them, and this effort has led to several cool innovations.

The first attack that comes to mind is probably the infamous 51 percent attack, but it's extremely expensive to execute and highly visible.[13] This concern tends to be followed by worries about "quantum," which we addressed at the end of chapter 1.

But the lesser-known eclipse attack is a much more pressing concern. Thwarting an attack like this is a cat-and-mouse game that we explore in chapters 7 and 8.

Another thing to worry about as a user is that the software you download doesn't outright steal your coins, and we'll go down that rabbit hole in chapter 9.

---

[13] Here are some charts that illustrate the difficulty of this attack: https://bitcoin.sipa.be ▣ The supply chain problems caused by chip shortages in 2020-2022 illustrate that even a well-resourced government can't easily get its hands on enough chips to attack the network.

Chapter 7

Eclipse Attacks

Ep. 17

An eclipse attack is a type of attack that isolates a Bitcoin node by occupying all of its connection slots to block the node from receiving any transactions and blocks, other than those sent to it by the attacker. This prevents the node from seeing what's going on in the Bitcoin network, and it potentially even tricks the node into accepting an alternative branch of the Bitcoin blockchain. Although nodes will never accept an invalid transaction or block, an eclipse attack can still cause harm, as we'll see.

This chapter discusses how this type of attack could be used to dupe users and miners. It also talks about solutions to counter this type of attack, some of which were outlined in the 2015 paper "Eclipse Attacks on Bitcoin's Peer-to-Peer Network," which was written by Ethan Heilman, Alison Kendler, Aviv Zohar, and Sharon Goldberg from Boston University and Hebrew University/MSR Israel.[1] Many of the solutions proposed by this paper have gradually been implemented in Bitcoin Core software in the past few years. This chapter also discusses some solutions that weren't in the paper.

---

[1] https://cs-people.bu.edu/heilman/eclipse/

Why an Eclipse Attack Hurts

Under normal circumstances, your node connects to the outside world via up to eight so-called "outbound peers." The outside world can also connect to you, and for that, your node allows a maximum of 117 inbound peers. In the case of an eclipse attack, your node only sees and connects to your attacker. So you might think you're talking to the whole world, but you're actually only talking to one person. In other words, that person is eclipsing your view of the world.

The reason you connect to all these nodes is because you want to ask them for new transactions and blocks. Data flows in both directions, no matter if the peer is inbound or outbound. Your peers may spontaneously send you blocks and transactions, and your node will in turn forward them to others. As long as you're connected to at least one honest peer, you won't miss out on the latest blocks and transactions.

An eclipse attack occurs if all of the peers you're connected to are controlled by a single entity, your attacker. Now they decide which blocks and transactions your node gets to see, and you may very well be missing out on the latest and greatest out there.

But why does this matter? They can't send you an invalid block with a fake signature that makes them a billionaire. Your node still checks all the rules and would never accept that. But what they can do is perform a double-spend attack on you.

So let's say you're expecting money from somebody, in this case from your attacker or someone they're colluding with,[2] and you see their transaction appear in your mempool

---

[2]In practice, victims often know who double-spent them. So, for example, it's not a good idea to double-spend an exchange if you just uploaded a copy of your passport. The author refers to this as proof-of-prison. This is probably why double-spend attacks are rare, even on

— which is where valid transactions wait to be confirmed —
but it's not yet in a block.

You might consider this payment complete and deliver
a product or service for it. But it turns out that, behind
your back, they sent an alternative transaction to the rest of
the network that *doesn't* pay you. This alternative, double-
spend[3] transaction gets included in a block, but your attacker
hides this block from you. So from your point of view, this
transaction is still in the mempool, and you remain oblivious
to the fact that you'll never truly receive these coins.

This is the most straightforward example of an eclipse attack. It's yet another reason that accepting zero-confirmation
transactions is a bad idea. Preventing double-spends is the
raison d'être for proof-of-work, so a transaction must be
included in a block in order to enjoy the protection of the
work in that block, and every block on top of it.

In the days before Bitcoin, the double-spend problem was
everywhere, and it was only considered solvable by introducing a trusted third party. For example, when receiving any
amount of Chaumian e-cash, the software on your computer
would immediately inform your bank that you received the
tokens. The bank's computer would then verify that these
tokens were never seen before. Without that step, the same
e-cash could've been spent to many different recipients.[4]

But even if you do wait for a confirmation, you're not out

---

altcoins with a much lower mining security budget than Bitcoin (we'll
get to the role of proof-of-work below).

[3]The thing that gets double-spent is one or more of the coins that
form the input for the transaction. A Bitcoin transaction takes coins as
its input and creates new coins as its output. An input can only ever
be spent once. When a node sees two transactions that spend the same
input, they have to pick one and ignore the other. The same goes for
miners, who decide which transaction candidate ends up in a block.

[4]Here's a brief explanation of Chaumian e-cash https://bitcoin.st
ackexchange.com/a/10666/4948 ▦. For a longer explanation and a
proposed Bitcoin-backed variation of it, listen to episode 52 of *Bitcoin,
Explained*: https://nadobtc.libsyn.com/federated-ecash-episode-52 ▦

of the woods. An eclipse attack is still possible, as we'll see, but it'll be a lot more expensive. This is because the attacker has to produce a valid block, and part of what determines the validity of a block is that it contains sufficient proof-of-work.

So let's say you sold something expensive. Like in the previous example, the attacker first sends you their transaction, and then they send a conflicting transaction to the rest of world, while making sure you never see it. That conflicting transaction gets confirmed, but your attacker doesn't forward this new block to you. Instead, they mine their own block with the original transaction in it. Your node tells you the transaction is confirmed, and you provide the goods or service.

Meanwhile, the outside world of normal miners keeps producing blocks, and the attacker continuous to hide those normal blocks from you. The attacker won't bother to produce any new blocks, because they have what they need from you. At some point, they stop the attack, or you figure out what happened and intervene. Either way, your node connects to legitimate peers again. It then learns about this longer chain that continued to grow during the attack. Even though, in this longer chain, you never got paid, your node switches to it anyway. In turn, the coins you received disappear.

A double-spend attack is also possible without an eclipse attack, but it's far less likely to succeed. First of all, you might notice the conflicting transaction in your own mempool and exercise additional caution before delivering any goods or services. And second, let's say an attacker controls 10 percent of hash power; their attack would fail 90 percent of the time, because the blocks they produce with the conflicting transaction all become stale.[5]

---

[5]When two blocks build on top of the same block, both are equally valid. As miners continue to generate more blocks, they'll pick one of those blocks to build on top of (usually whichever they saw first). Eventually, the tie is broken and one chain becomes longer. The block

If you wait for two confirmations, the odds for your attacker drop to 1 percent. This is a good reminder of why it's important for Bitcoin to be somewhat expensive, so that it's not too easy to produce blocks on alternative branches that double-spend coins. Back in 2015, when the paper we mentioned above was written, these attacks were a lot cheaper: $5,000–$10,000 per block.[6] So, the attacker is only going to attack you if the cost of making a fake block is lower than the amount of money they're scamming you for. Note that, in practice, someone can't just order a tailormade block for their attack, unless they *are* a miner. Since any double-spend attack would harm Bitcoin's reputation, which would reduce miner revenue, they aren't particularly incentivized to facilitate such attacks.[7]

Producing a block costs money, mainly for equipment and electricity. An honest miner recoups this by selling or borrowing against the coins created in the coinbase transaction. This is the first transaction in every block, and it has special rules. The first rule is that, unlike regular transactions, a coinbase transaction doesn't have inputs. It creates money out of nowhere, but the amount is capped by the sum of the block subsidy (currently 6.25 BTC and halving every four years) and all the fees paid by transactions included in

---

that's now no longer part of the longest chain is called stale. The website https://forkmonitor.info/ keeps track of these events and shows an alert as soon as two blocks appear at the same height. It also keeps track of how many blocks are built on each side, until one side falls behind and becomes stale.

[6]https://bitcoinvisuals.com/chain-block-reward

[7]However, when the same equipment can be used to mine multiple coins, then causing some reputation damage on one coin leaves plenty of other coins to mine. There are platforms where people can rent hash power, and those have sometimes been used to perform a double-spend attack. Especially when a coin enjoys very little hash power, such an attack can be very cheap. See e.g. https://www.coindesk.com/marke ts/2020/08/07/ethereum-classic-attacker-successfully-double-spends-168m-in-second-attack-report/

the block. The output side of the transaction sends this to wherever the miner wants, but usually an address managed by a mining pool, which then redistributes it.

Normally, a miner produces a block that builds on top of the most recently mined block that they're aware of. And the coinbase transaction has a second special rule,[8] enforced by all nodes, which says that it can't be spent until it has 101 confirmations, i.e. until there are 101 blocks built on top of it. This is called coinbase maturity.[9]

The attacker doesn't care about the coinbase reward, because they stand to make more from scamming you (hypothetically). Instead of building on top of the most recent block out there, they create a block on top of the last block *you* know of. And they don't broadcast this block to the world, so no other miners will mine on top of it. This means their coinbase transaction never reaches maturity, so the costs of producing the block can't be recouped directly. It makes no economic sense for a miner to do this, unless they directly benefit from the attack... or unless they're duped, as we explain below.

It turns out an attacker can also use miners against you without their cooperation by trying to split miners. They do this by not just eclipsing you, but also by eclipsing one or more miners. The eclipsed miners, presumably a minority, would see the same transaction as you, the actual target victim. Once they mine it, the attacker ensures that your node is the only one that gets to see this block. This miner is a victim too, because just like your transaction ends up disappearing once the block eventually goes stale, their coinbase transaction disappears too. For all this economic damage, the attacker might only rob you of $100. So we really want eclipse attacks to be very difficult.

---

[8] As an aside, as we explained in chapter 3, SegWit imposes a third special rule on the coinbase transaction: It needs to contain an `OP_RETURN` output with a hash of the witness data for the block.

[9] https://bitcoin.stackexchange.com/a/1992/4948

Miners and pool operators are of course not naive. They might run multiple nodes in different countries and take precautions so that an attacker won't know which node to eclipse. In addition, mining is still somewhat centralized, so there are specialized networks that connect them, making eclipse attacks even more difficult.[10] But this shouldn't be the only thing we're relying on to prevent these attacks. Luckily, more and more improvements that are designed to make these attacks more difficult are being deployed.

How an Eclipse Attack Works

So far we've assumed that an eclipse attack can be done, in order to explain how it's used to trick you into parting with your hard-earned coins. But how is it actually done?

Recall from above that, in order to eclipse your node, the attacker needs to take over all eight of your outbound connections and whatever number of inbound connections your node has. This is a cat and mouse game, and even before the above-mentioned paper was written, the Bitcoin Core software was hardened to prevent eclipse attacks. But let's see how the paper proposed overcoming the existing defenses.

There are a couple of ingredients. First, as mentioned in chapter 2, when a node starts, it tries to find other peers, and once it's been running for a while, it has a list of addresses it learned from other peers and it stores them in a file. Then, whenever a node loses one of its eight outbound connections, or when it restarts, it looks at this file with all the addresses it's ever heard of, and it starts randomly connecting to them.

---

[10]One such network to connect miners is the Fast Internet Bitcoin Relay Engine (FIBRE): https://bitcoin.stackexchange.com/questions/ 56485/can-someone-please-explain-fibre-to-me-like-im-5-and-why-is-it-useful

As an attacker, the idea is to pollute this file by giving your node a bunch of addresses that either don't exist or that they (the attacker) control. This way, whatever address your node picks, every time it makes a connection, it either fails because there's nothing there, or it connects to the attacker — and eventually all connections are to the attacker.

The attacker also needs to control all inbound connections to your node. Without going into too much detail in this chapter, one approach is to just make lots and lots of connection attempts until all your 117 inbound slots are full. Over time, perhaps weeks, as honest peers occasionally disconnect from you, the attacker quickly fills the open inbound slots so that no new honest peers get through.[11]

As early as 2012, developers realized it was possible for an attacker to give your node huge numbers of IP addresses, all controlled by them. Let's say your node has 1,000 real IP addresses of other nodes. Then the attacker feeds you 9,000 addresses that they control. As your node starts to pick IP addresses, the odds are 90 percent that it will connect to the attacker.

But as long as these addresses were closely related, e.g. because they were all in the same data center, there was something that could be done. A bucket system was introduced, and it puts all IP addresses with the same two starting digits, e.g. `172.67.*.*` into the same bucket. The node would then pick from different buckets for each of its outbound connections.[12]

In the example above, all the attacker's IP addresses end up in one bucket, and there are 256 such buckets, so the odds of connecting to even a single attacker node drop dramatically. Keep in mind that you only need *one* honest

---

[11]This has been made more difficult by sometimes dropping an existing inbound connection in favor of a new one: https://github.com /bitcoin/bitcoin/pull/6374

[12]https://github.com/bitcoin/bitcoin/pull/787

peer to be protected against eclipse attacks.

Each bucket is also limited in size, so most of the 9,000 addresses in the example above would be thrown out of their bucket almost as soon as they entered it.

Finally, in the same pull request, nodes also started remembering which nodes they previously connected to. Whenever they needed a new connection, they would toss a coin, and either connect to one of those, or pick a new one from one of the 256 buckets.

The Botnet

You might think this would do the trick, but here's where the paper comes into play. The authors ran a simulation to see how difficult it was to actually overflow all these buckets, and it found that, within a matter of days, it can be successful.

How did they do this? By using a botnet[13] — not a real one of course, as that would probably be unethical for university researchers, not to mention potentially illegal. But they simulated one. A botnet is a group of random computers in the world that have been hacked and can be remote controlled. Because they're not all in the same data center as our example above, their IP addresses have many different starting digits, so they end up in different buckets.

The paper estimated that a botnet with less than 5,000 computers can successfully pull off an eclipse attack. That might sound like a big botnet, but you can rent that from various nefarious "companies" for less than $100.[14]

In addition to attacking your node from many different directions, thereby defeating the bucket system, the hypothetical attacker in the paper also exploited other weaknesses.

---

[13]https://en.wikipedia.org/wiki/Botnet

[14]Business Model of a Botnet: https://arxiv.org/pdf/1804.10848.pdf

First, they would flood your node with IP addresses that are known to be fake. This would flush all buckets with fake nodes. Remember that when your node needs a new peer, it'll toss a coin to either connect to familiar node or try a new one. Well, there wouldn't be any new ones to try.[15]

For the other side of the coin flip — connecting to a familiar node — the attackers exploited another weakness. It turns out your node considers any node it ever connected to "familiar." That includes botnet nodes that connected *to* it, even if only briefly.[16] There's a separate 64-bucket system for these familiar nodes, and over time, they get filled up by botnet IPs.

Don't Crash

At this point, your node still has long-lived connections to the real world from before the attack began, so the attacker still needs to get rid of those. The trick is to either wait for your node to restart, or to try and crash it.

Whenever your node restarts,[17] it starts out with zero connections. Firstly, this creates an opportunity to very quickly fill up all 117 inbound slots. And secondly, it's going to look at that file of peers it knows, and it's going to try and connect to them. If an attacker succeeded at dominating these buckets, your node is exclusively going to connect to attacker IP addresses. That's all that's needed for the eclipse attack to be in play.

So although crashing a Bitcoin node isn't a very useful attack on its own, it can help when performing an eclipse

---

[15]We'll revisit the problem of fake nodes in chapter 8.

[16]Fixed in 2016: https://github.com/bitcoin/bitcoin/pull/8594 ▣

[17]Nodes that run on a server are typically automatically restarted after a crash or system reboot, using something like systemd: https://en.wikipedia.org/wiki/Systemd ▣

attack. This is one reason why it's important for developers to ensure they don't write code that can make a node crash.

How to Solve It

It's important to understand that attacks like these are a numbers game. An attacker needs to give your node a lot of spam addresses to fill up all the buckets and make sure it only connects to you.

So one obvious mitigation[18] of an attack like this is to have more buckets. Unfortunately, this doesn't help much with isolation, because doubling the number of buckets only doubles the attack cost,[19] and we already saw how cheap it is. Still, the number of buckets was quadrupled almost immediately after the paper was published.[20]

Another countermeasure lies in the aforementioned coin toss. This toss was actually biased toward trying new nodes and toward those that your node most recently learned about. This was changed to just a coin toss (in that same early pull request). Why not go further and only connect to peers your node has known the longest? There are always tradeoffs — in this case, your node might spend too much time going through a list of no-longer-reachable IP addresses.

But there was another proposed mitigation that also provided a bias toward familiar nodes, only in a safer way. It pertained to how buckets are handled when they're about

---

[18]mitigate — "to cause to become less harsh or hostile": https://www.merriam-webster.com/dictionary/mitigate
A mitigation isn't a complete solution. Although a bit redundant, the term "partial mitigation" is often used as well.

[19]$O(n)$: The cost of an attack grows linearly with the number of buckets (n). A much stronger defense is something that increases the cost of an attack quadratically - $O(n^2)$ - or even exponentially. https://www.freecodecamp.org/news/big-o-notation-why-it-matters-and-why-it-doesnt-1674cfa8a23c/

[20]https://github.com/bitcoin/bitcoin/pull/5941/commits/1d21ba2 f5ecbf03086d0b65c4c4c80a39a94c2ee

to overflow. When you hear of a new address and you want to put it in a bucket and remove something else, you first check the address that's already in the bucket. That entails connecting to it to see if it still exists. If it does exist, you don't replace it. This is called a feeler connection. This was more complicated and it took until mid-2016 to be implemented.[21]

Still, other mitigations took much longer. When Bitcoin Core 0.21.0 was released in January 2021, it included a new method to prevent eclipse attacks that was suggested in this same 2015 paper: the use of anchor connections.[22] What happens is that when you restart, you try to remember some of the last connections you had. Your node remembers the two connections that it only exchanges blocks with, and it tries to reconnect to those.

Why two? It's not a good idea to always try to reconnect to the same nodes again when you restart, as, for all you know, the reason you crashed in the first place is because one of those nodes was evil. The same logic applies to the scenario where you're *already* being eclipsed.[23]

What Else Can Be Done?

In addition to the many suggestions from the paper, there are other things that can be done, and some have been implemented.

You may be wondering: Why wouldn't you just have as many connections as possible from the get-go? But the problem is that it requires a lot of data exchange — especially for the transactions in a mempool — and that's extremely data

---

[21]By one of the authors in fact: https://github.com/bitcoin/bitcoin /pull/8282

[22]https://github.com/bitcoin/bitcoin/pull/17428

[23]https://github.com/bitcoin/bitcoin/issues/17326#issuecommen t-550521262

intensive, so you can't just add more connections without also increasing bandwidth use.

Erlay (see appendix A) is a proposal for reducing the bandwidth needed for these mempool synchronizations. It reduces the main cost (bandwidth) *per connection*. A lower cost per connection allows nodes to have more connections. Having more connections makes any eclipse attack scheme more difficult.

Another way to have more connections without increasing bandwidth too much is to constrain some connections to blocks only, and to not sync the mempool with those peers. This was implemented in 2019.[24]

Finally, there's the Blockstream Satellite,[25] or any other satellite or even radio broadcast.[26] These allow anyone in the world to receive the latest blocks. This is mainly useful for people with very low bandwidth internet connections in remote areas. But it can also offer protection against an eclipse attack. This is because when your node receives the satellite signal, even if all inbound and outbound connections are taken over by an attacker, you'll still learn about new blocks.

Note, however, that you shouldn't blindly trust the satellite either, for *it* might try to eclipse you. But remember that you only need a single honest peer, and you achieve this by having as diverse a set of connections as possible.

The Bitcoin Core development wiki also contains an overview of eclipse attacks and various counter measures.[27]

---

[24]https://github.com/bitcoin/bitcoin/pull/15759

[25]https://blockstream.com/satellite/

[26]https://www.wired.com/story/cypherpunks-bitcoin-ham-radio/

[27]https://github.com/bitcoin-core/bitcoin-devwiki/wiki/Addrman-and-eclipse-attacks

Erebus Attack

Ep. 18

If you want to learn more about eclipse attacks, you might be interested in the Erebus attack[28]: an eclipse attack where an attacker essentially spoofs an entire part of the internet.

How this works is the internet is made up of Autonomous Systems (AS), which are basically clusters of IP addresses owned by the same entity, like an ISP.[29]

As it turns out, however, some Autonomous Systems can effectively act as bottlenecks when trying to reach other Autonomous Systems. This allows an attacker controlling such a bottleneck to launch a successful eclipse attack — even against nodes that connect with multiple Autonomous Systems.

As explained above, Bitcoin Core nodes already counter eclipse attacks by ensuring they're connected to a variety of IP addresses, based on the first two digits of the IP address. This can be further improved by separating buckets by Autonomous Systems instead.

But this doesn't thwart the Erebus attack. For that, recent versions of Bitcoin Core include an optional feature — ASMAP.[30]

The episode explains how mapping the internet has allowed Bitcoin Core contributors to create a tool which ensures that Bitcoin nodes not only connect to various Autonomous Systems, but also that they avoid being trapped behind said bottlenecks.

---

[28]https://erebus-attack.comp.nus.edu.sg

[29]https://www.cloudflare.com/learning/network-layer/what-is-an-autonomous-system/

[30]https://blog.bitmex.com/call-to-action-testing-and-improving-asmap/

Chapter 8

Fake Nodes

Ep. 49

This chapter talks about an attack that took place in the summer of 2021. It discusses what happened, speculates why it may have happened, and shares the fix that will prevent it from happening again.

Random Connections

In mid 2021, people who run nodes started noticing that random people were connecting to them.[1] This, on its own, is perfectly normal. As we explained in chapter 2, it's part of how nodes bootstrap to the network. They randomly connect to nodes and ask for addresses of more nodes to connect to. They also announce their own IP, which gets gossiped around, so soon enough, the node will receive inbound connections.

However, what was unusual in this instance was these random people would connect to them and then send 500

---

[1]To read the thread where people mention noticing this attack, see https://bitcointalk.org/index.php?topic=5348856.0

messages,[2] and each of those 500 messages would contain 10
IP addresses that were supposed to represent other nodes in
the network. After that, they'd just disconnect. It certainly
didn't seem dangerous, but it wasn't the usual behavior.

Although the messages were perfectly valid, their contents was nonsense, because the IP addresses these nodes
sent were just randomly generated numbers. You could tell
this if you mapped them out; the pattern would match that
of randomly generated numbers. Another way you could tell
is because the list would contain IP addresses that simply
can't exist for various reasons, e.g. because they're reserved
for private networks such as 192.168.0.1.

The problem with these randomly generated IP addresses
is that, if you're flooded with them, they make it almost
impossible to connect to a real node. There are less than
a hundred thousand nodes out there that your node can
connect to, yet there are four billion IPv4 addresses. The
purpose of the address gossip protocol is exactly to prevent
this random guessing. But this attack wasn't big enough to
flood individual nodes.

As people looked into this more, they discovered it was
happening on a fairly large scale, classifying it as an attack.
In reality, this kind of attack isn't a big problem for an individual node, especially if it already has lots of IP addresses
from honest nodes. It might connect to a few nodes that
don't exist, but it's mostly a waste of time and resources,
since it's connecting to and storing IP addresses that aren't
real Bitcoin node IP addresses. So on the individual level,
it's like a kid throwing a little pebble at you.

Furthermore, we know it wasn't a big deal just from the
fact that hardly anyone even noticed what was happening.
But it does deserve investigation.

---

[2]https://developer.bitcoin.org/reference/p2p_networking.html#a
ddr

Why Would Someone Attack?

A couple weeks after this attack, Matthias Grundmann and Max Baumstark wrote a paper[3] describing the attack and speculating about the reasoning behind it.

What they're guessing is that this attacker wasn't so much trying to destroy the network, as they were trying to map the network to get a sense of how well nodes are connected to each other. And the reason they can do that is because when you receive 10 IP addresses, you'll forward each of them to exactly two of your peers.[4]

If the attacker also connects to you using a regular (not spamming) node, it'll receive some fraction of the spam address that you forward. From that fraction, it can calculate how many peers you have. More generally, in a surveillance attack like this, it's like they're monitoring the echo of their own attack. By looking at this echo, they can determine a little bit of what the network looks like, including the shape of it, how well connected it is, how robust it is, etc. This information could potentially be used for future attacks, or it could just be for research purposes.

Defense Mechanisms

There are some existing defense mechanisms in nodes that make it more difficult to use this information. For example, if you're telling a node a bunch of IP addresses, it's not going to immediately connect to all of them — not only because that would make it too easy to invite a node into connecting to a trap, but also because, most of the time, a node already has sufficient connections. It also doesn't relay all of them,

---

[3]https://arxiv.org/abs/2108.00815

[4]It won't propagate further. Although you received these spam addresses in neat packages of 10, your node will forward them in bigger packages. Nodes don't forward any addresses in a package if it was bigger than 10, so the attack fizzles out after just two hops.

and for those addresses that are relayed, there's a random time delay. So, it makes it very difficult to say specifically which node connects to which node connects to which node.

These defense mechanisms are added to Bitcoin Core incrementally, often as a defense against eclipse attacks, as we explained in chapter 7. Essentially, when people do these types of attacks — probing the network in weird ways — experienced developers and security researchers will look at them and see how they can add something against them.

In this instance, they added a counter measure.[5] Normally, when people are acting nice, they'll connect to you and send you one IP address — namely their own. Occasionally, they'll send you some other IP addresses, but not very frequently — the average node will share an IP address with a peer maybe once every 20 seconds.

Because an attacker will send addresses at a much higher rate, the counter measure is to introduce a rate limiter. This basically says, "OK, when a new node connects to me, I'll allow it to send me one address immediately, and then I'll allow up to one address every 20 seconds." It tracks how many seconds have gone by, and if the node is sending too many addresses, it'll ignore the new ones that go over the rate limit. So the "attackers" don't get punished, but rather ignored.[6]

Of course, there are cases where nodes actually want to receive lots of addresses from their peers. For example, if somebody connects to you and you say, "Please tell me addresses, and give me up to 1,000," then of course the response won't be rate limited. In such a scenario, you'll make sure that they can actually give you those addresses, but if it's unsolicited, then you rate limit it.

---

[5]https://github.com/bitcoin/bitcoin/pull/22387 ▨

[6]Overzealously punishing bad behavior can lead to network partitioning, which is something that an attacker could even exploit by tricking regular nodes into "angering" their peers and getting themselves disconnected.

Responsible Disclosure

Now, what's really interesting is that this fix was published in the weeks *before* the attack happened. It wasn't merged into Bitcoin Core yet, but rather just an open pull request, or proposed change. It remained open until shortly after the attack, but then it was merged and released in version 22.0.

So it almost sounds like somebody saw the solution and saw an opportunity to carry out this specific attack. Or perhaps somebody was already planning this attack and then figured they should do it soon, before it was no longer possible.

For more on this attack and related issues, there's also a great Chaincode Labs podcast episode.[7]

There have been other examples of a situation where publishing a fix may itself have caused the attack. Back in the day, there was an alternative node implementation Bitcoin Unlimited. It had a bug that was fixed, but before the fix was deployed, the bug was exploited by somebody. That attack brought down all the Bitcoin Unlimited nodes at that time.[8]

Additionally, around 2013, something similar didn't happen, but could've happened, on Bitcoin, which we covered in chapter 4. This is because the OpenSSL library was made stricter in its software by imposing constraints on signatures. Had it been discovered only a few months later, after a Bitcoin Core release was already out there with the bug in it, then it would've been a zero-day situation. Perhaps in that case, the fix would've been disguised as nice cleanup software, rather than a patch for a security vulnerability. If someone had found out, they could've posted a slightly

---

[7]From 23:15 "Rate limiting on address gossip": https://podcast.ch aincode.com/2021/10/26/pieter-wuille-amiti-uttarwar-p2p.html

[8]https://bitcoinmagazine.com/technical/security-researcher-found-bug-knocked-out-bitcoin-unlimited

different kind of signature and caused a fork because some nodes would accept it and other nodes wouldn't accept it.

A final example is that of an inflation bug in 2018.[9] It was presented as a fix to a bug that will crash your node. And that was true — it could crash your node — but it could also create inflation. The latter fact was a bit more important, and it was of course not announced, because somebody could've exploited it in that window of opportunity.

One way to handle scenarios like this is for developers to pretend that something isn't a big deal until people have actually downloaded and used the fix — and then to reveal only later that it was actually a much bigger problem they were fixing. This makes it less likely that an attacker detects the vulnerability while it's still exploitable.

But that's really not an ideal approach, because in open source development, you want to be very transparent about things you're changing. Because if you're not being transparent about fixing a critical bug, then maybe you're also not transparent about adding inflation. It's a delicate balance.

---

[9]https://bitcoincore.org/en/2018/09/20/notice/

Chapter 9

Why Open Source Matters — Guix

Ep. 21

This chapter discusses open source software in the context of why it matters that Bitcoin software is open source. But it also delves into the reason why even open source software doesn't necessarily solve all software-specific trust issues.

In theory, the fact that most Bitcoin nodes, wallets, and applications are open source should ensure that developers can't include malicious code in the programs, because anyone can inspect the source code for malware. In practice, however, the number of people with enough expertise to do this is limited, while the reliance by software in general on external code libraries, or dependencies, makes it even harder.

Furthermore, even if the open source code is sound, this doesn't guarantee that the binaries (computer code) really correspond with the open source code. The first attempt at mitigating this risk in Bitcoin involved a process called Gitian building. This is where several Bitcoin Core developers sign the binaries if, and only if, they all produce the exact same binaries from the same source code. This requires special compiler software.

More recently, Guix, a project that goes above and beyond the Gitian process, came along. It helped minimize the level of trust required to turn source code into binaries — including trust in the compiler itself.

Free vs. Open Source

Before getting into the details of Gitian and Guix, this section serves as a brief primer on the historical difference between free software and open source software and how they were combined into FOSS (free and open-source software).

The idea behind the free software movement is that if software is closed source, it results in a power relationship between developers and users, because users don't know what software they're running.

The actual software as it's read by your computer is written in a language no human can understand, a binary format made up of ones and zeros. But when humans wrote that software, they used a programming language, such as C++. These two aren't the same thing, even if most mortals can't read either. So when you're running closed software, all you have access to is this binary, not the programming language used to produce it. As a result, you have no idea what your computer is doing.

So, for example, if a developer puts malware into the closed software, your computer could spy on you or do something you don't actually want the software to do, and you wouldn't be able to see it.

A programmer by the name of Richard Stallman didn't like the idea of closed software, so he started the free software movement, which specified that source code had to be available so people could actually check what they were running on their computers. This in turn eliminated the power dynamic. So, free in that context means freedom; it doesn't mean free as in free beer.

A slightly different, but compatible, perspective was given by Eric S. Raymond in his 1999 book *The Cathedral and the Bazaar: Musings on Linux and Open Source by an Accidental Revolutionary*.[1] In it, he explained the benefits of free software and how it could actually provide high-quality code. According to him, "given enough eyeballs, all bugs are shallow." In other words, the more a piece of code is seen and reviewed, the better the chance all its bugs are found.

Because of this pragmatic reasoning about code quality, the people at the Netscape Communications Corporation were convinced to turn their internal browser into an open source project, Mozilla. We're calling it open source now because this group of people rebranded free software to open source (to prevent any confusion with beer). And that's where the difference between free software and open source stems from.

Bitcoin, an Open Source Project

Now, the question is how all of this is connected to Bitcoin. Here's an example. When you run a piece of wallet software, it will display an address. What if it turns out that address doesn't belong to you, but instead it's controlled by the developer? Then every time someone pays you, the coins don't go to you. This is why you really need maximum transparency of what exactly is running on your machine.

One thing you can do, if you have the skill, is to compile the wallet software yourself, thereby avoiding the need to download an untrusted binary. That doesn't solve the problem for the vast majority of users though. It also doesn't entirely solve the problem for you, because even if you can

---

[1]https://en.wikipedia.org/wiki/The_Cathedral_and_the_Bazaar

see the code in its original programming language, it's hard to understand exactly what it's going to do once it runs on your computer. For one thing, it's simply too much code for one person to understand.

That's why you want whatever Bitcoin code is running to be open source — so as many people as possible can see what it is. Remember that given enough eyeballs, all bugs are shallow, and the same goes for detecting malicious pieces of code.

Bitcoin code is open source and it's hosted on GitHub in a repository. This means anyone with the know-how can look at the source code and check that it does what it's supposed to do. But in reality, the number of people who can actually do that and understand it is limited.[2] Though occasionally, they even get some help from developers who work on altcoins.[3]

---

[2]The number of people who can read this code depends on what you mean by actually read. How many people are computer literate in general? How many can roughly read what a C++ program is doing? Probably tens of millions (https://redmonk.com/jgovernor/2017/05/ 26/just-how-many-darned-developers-are-there-in-the-world-github-is-puzzled/ 🔲). But of those, perhaps only a few thousand have ever worked on cryptocurrency or similar software. There are dozens of active developers on any given day who all look at the code. But none of them can oversee all the changes in the entire project, because that requires specialization: One developer might know everything about peer-to-peer networking code and absolutely nothing about wallet code.

[3]For example, the very serious CVE-2018-17144 was found by Bitcoin Cash developer Awemany (https://bitcoinops.org/en/topics/cve-2018-17144/ 🔲). Many altcoin projects started by copy-pasting the Bitcoin source code and then changing a few things to differentiate themselves. For example, Dogecoin changed the inflation schedule, decreased the time between blocks, and used a different proof-of-work algorithm. But that still left 99% of its codebase identical to Bitcoin Core: Digital signatures are checked the same way, transactions and blocks are verified the same way, the peer-to-peer network works the same way, etc. So when altcoin developers are working on their projects, they may discover bugs in that 99% of the codebase they share with Bitcoin Core. This adds to the security of Bitcoin.

If we wanted to increase the number of people who could read and understand Bitcoin source code, it'd need to be cleaner and more readable, because the original code Satoshi wrote was very, very hard to reason about.[4]

Checking the Validity

Let's say you trust the development and release process, so you download the binary from bitcoincore.org. The first problem is that you don't know if bitcoincore.org is run by the Bitcoin developers. But even if you were confident of that, it could be that the site is hacked, or the site isn't hacked, but the DNS is hacked. There are many ways in which you could end up downloading malware.

To get around this, open source projects almost always publish a checksum, which is a sequence of numbers and letters. What this means is that if you download something and run a particular script on it, the resulting checksum you get should match what the developers say it should be. The project maintainer usually publishes the checksum on the download page. In theory, that works. However, whoever hacked the site might have also hacked the checksum, so it's not foolproof.

The next step is to sign the checksum. So, for example, a well-known person — in this case, Wladimir van der Laan, the (Dutch) lead maintainer[5] of Bitcoin Core — signs the

---

[4]To understand what it means to reason about something, imagine you're looking at code and you see there's a function called "make a private key." Your line of thinking might go as follows: "OK, what does that function do? Oh, it calls in this other function. Where's that other function? Oh, it's 20,000 lines up in the same file. Let me scroll 20,000 lines up and have a look at that code. I see, it's referring to a variable. Oh, but this variable is also accessed in 15 different places in the codebase..."

[5]Maintainers aren't as powerful as some people think they are: https://blog.lopp.net/who-controls-bitcoin-core-/

Also, as of recently, multiple developers sign the release checksum.

checksum using a PGP key that's publicly known. It's been the same for 10 years. So assuming you weren't fooled the first time, whenever you download an updated version, you know which PGP key the checksums ought to be signed with.

Why trust him? Well, he knows the binaries reflect the open source code because he took the source code, ran a command, and got the binary. In other words, he put the code through some other piece of software that produces binaries from the open source software.

But how do you know he actually did that? Here's where it gets a little bit more complicated. Ideally, what you do is you run the same command and you also compile it, and then hopefully, you get the same result.

Sometimes that works with a specific project, but as the project gets complicated, it often doesn't work, because what the exact binary file is going to be depends on some very specific details on your computer system.

Take a trivial C++ program:

```
int main() {
  return 0;
}
```

This program exits and returns 0. It's more boring than "Hello, World!"[6]

Say you compile this on a Mac and it produces a 16,536-byte program. When you repeat that on a different Mac, it produces an identical file, as evidenced by its SHA-256[7] checksum. But when you compile it on an Ubuntu machine, you get a 15,768-byte result.

All it takes is one changed letter in a computer program, or in its compiled binary, and boom, your checksum doesn't work anymore.

---

[6]https://en.wikipedia.org/wiki/%22Hello,_World!%22_program

[7]https://en.wikipedia.org/wiki/SHA-2

If the compiled program includes a library (see chapter 4), then the end result depends on the exact library version that happened to be on the developer machine when they created the binary.

So when you download the latest Bitcoin Core from its website and you compare it to what you compiled yourself, it's going to have a different checksum. Perhaps the difference is due to you having a more recent version of some library, or perhaps it's due to a subtle difference between your system and Wladimir's.

As mentioned above, if you're one of those lucky people who can compile code yourself, this isn't a big deal. What's more likely, however, is that your security depends on the hope that somebody else will do this check for you. Those people might then sound the alarm if anything is wrong.

But because it's so difficult to check if the source code matches the downloadable binary, should you really assume that anyone out there does this?

Fixing the Problem with Gitian

In order to verify no shenanigans happened in the process of converting source code to a compiled binary, you need something called reproducible builds, or deterministic builds.

What deterministic implies is that, given a source, you're going to get the same binary. And if you change one letter in the source, you're going to get a different binary, but everybody will get the same result if they make the same change.

In addition, there's the problem of slight differences in machine configuration leading to a different binary file.

Until mid 2021, the way Bitcoin Core did this was with Gitian.[8] In short, you'd take a virtual or physical computer,

---

[8]https://gitian.org/

download the installation DVD[9] for a very specific Ubuntu version, and install that. This ensures everyone has an identical starting position, and because Ubuntu is widely used, there's some confidence that there isn't a Bitcoin backdoor on the installation disk.

Inside that machine, you build another virtual machine, which has been tailormade to ensure it builds identical binaries for everyone using it. For example, it uses a fixed fake time so that if a timestamp ends up in the final binary, it's going to be the same timestamp no matter what time you ran the compiler. It ensures all the libraries are the exact same versions, it uses a very specific compiler version, etc. And then you build Bitcoin Core inside that virtual machine and look at the checksum. This should now match the downloadable files on bitcoincore.org.

About a dozen developers and other volunteers run this "computer within a computer." Around each new released version, they all compile the binaries and publish the resulting hashes for others to see. In addition, they sign these hashes with their public PGP keys.

However, while this sounds easy in theory, in practice, it's always been a huge pain to get the system working. There aren't many open source projects that use Gitian — as far as we know, only Bitcoin Core and Tor do. Even most, if not all, altcoin forks of the Bitcoin Core software don't bother with this process.

---

[9]Long ago you might have ordered a CD by snail mail, whereas nowadays, you'll probably download an image and put it on a USB stick. When you install Ubuntu on a virtual machine, your computer creates a virtual DVD player using the image. https://ubuntu.com/download/server

Dependencies, Dependencies, Dependencies

However, this isn't the only problem.

Let's say you just read the Facebook terms and conditions, but it turns out those terms and conditions point to some other document — perhaps the entirety of US copyright law. So now you have to read that too.

Similarly, just reviewing the Bitcoin Core code isn't enough, because like most computer programs, it uses all sorts of other things, known as dependencies, mostly in the form of libraries (see chapter 4). And each library might in turn use some other library, and so forth and so on. So you need to inspect all of those too.

One of the constraints Bitcoin Core developers work with is to keep the number of dependencies as small as possible, and also to not update them all the time. Such updates require extra review work. And of course, the people who maintain those dependencies know Bitcoin Core is using them; all the more reason to be somewhat on your toes to make sure that those projects are being scrutinized, too.

And if it turns out that a dependency is corrupt, it could steal your coins. This actually happened in at least one other project in 2018. It involved a dependency of a dependency of a dependency of the Copay wallet. Fortunately, it was detected quickly,[10] so it was never exploited in the wild.

---

[10]What happened was they had a piece of software that's open source, meaning everybody could review it. But it used dependencies, and those dependencies used dependencies, and so on.

They were using npm, which is the package manager for Node.js. This is, in turn, a large open source community, and it's a highly modular system.

Every single package links to a repository on GitHub, with its own maintainer who can release updates whenever they want. A typical piece of wallet software might be pulling in 10,000 dependencies indirectly. You might start with five dependencies, and each of those pull in 50 dependencies, and those each pull in another 50 dependencies. If even

A more recent example of casual dependency usage gone horribly wrong is the Log4j saga.[11]

The Solution

This begs the questions of what the solution is, and unfortunately, it's to not depend on dependencies. If unavoidable, it's important to use as few as possible, and you especially want to stay away from things that have nested dependencies.

In the case of Bitcoin Core, it's not too bad, because it doesn't have many dependencies, and those dependencies don't have a lot of nested ones. So, it's not a big tree. It's relatively shallow, and you'd have to go after those specific dependencies directly to attack.

Who Builds the Builder?

Earlier in this chapter, we discussed how Gitian helps create deterministic builds. But what if Gitian, or any of the tools it uses, is itself corrupted somehow?

For example, since Gitian uses Ubuntu, somebody might say, "Hey, this Bitcoin project's pretty cool. This Ubuntu project's pretty cool. Let me contribute some source to Ubuntu." Their "contribution" could be a small change to the compiler that's shipped with Ubuntu. They could modify that compiler, so that whenever it compiles Bitcoin, it sneaks

---

a single one of the developers or maintainers of any of these packages is corrupted, they could include coin-stealing malware.

A JavaScript wallet like Copay stores a user's private keys somewhere inside the browser memory. Unfortunately, that's a very egalitarian place, meaning that any piece of JavaScript can access it. This is how malware hidden in a sub-sub-dependency can steal coins.

For more information, see this writeup: https://www.synopsys.com/blogs/software-security/malicious-dependency-supply-chain/

[11]https://english.ncsc.nl/topics/log4j-vulnerability

in some code to steal coins, but when it compiles any other software, it behaves normally.

This example is a bit contrived, and someone attempting this is very likely to get caught long before they do any damage; there's much more scrutiny on compiler software and on Ubuntu than there is in for example the Node.js ecosystem we mentioned above. But the general attack strategy would be the same. And with a trillion dollars at stake, attackers can be very sophisticated and very patient.

Now let's say everybody runs their Gitian builder, which includes this hypothetical compromised Ubuntu compiler. It would be very, very scary, because it'd still have deterministic builds, because everybody is using the exact same malware to build it.

There are two kinds of dependencies: One is the dependency you're actively running that's inside the binary you're shipping to your customers. But the other dependency, and it's no less a can of worms, is all the tools you're using to produce the binary, and even to download the binary.

So if even a single one of the tools that developers use to build Bitcoin Core is corrupt, deterministic builds won't help. Every developer running the Gitian build process would diligently produce the same malware. The binary will not match what's in the source code.

The hope is that the people who are maintaining all these compilers and all the other things know what they're doing and would never let any backdoor through. This isn't just a problem for Bitcoin users. The entire world relies on this scrutiny, which is mostly done by volunteers.

So can we do better?

Enter Guix

The key is to make everything open source and everything a deterministic build. Every library, every printer driver, every compiler — everything. For Bitcoin Core to truly be a deterministic build, each of its dependencies needs to be a deterministic build, as does every tool that's used to build it, including the compiler. Ideally the hardware is as well, but that's a whole other can of worms.[12]

This is where Guix[13] enters the picture. This GNU project has been around for a decade, but a few years ago, Carl Dong[14] from Chaincode Labs[15] began work on replacing Gitian with Guix, which finally happened in Bitcoin Core version 22.[16] This involved making changes on both the Bitcoin Core and the Guix side of things.

The ambition of Guix is roughly as follows:[17] You start with a few hundred bytes of actual machine code. That's the binary code that you must trust.[18] From there on, all it does is read source code and compile it. But how do you do that when there isn't a compiler?

Well, this first binary blob performs a bootstrap.[19] It's

---

[12]https://media.ccc.de/v/36c3-10690-open_source_is_insufficient _to_solve_trust_problems_in_hardware 🔲

[13]https://guix.gnu.org/ 🔲

[14]https://twitter.com/carl_dong 🔲

[15]https://chaincode.com/ 🔲

[16]https://bitcoin.org/en/releases/22.0/ 🔲

[17]See also Carl Dong's presentation: https://www.youtube.com/wa tch?v=I2iShmUTEl8 🔲

[18]Even binary code can be seen as source code. It's simply a series of instructions for the CPU. And this particular machine code is well documented: https://git.savannah.nongnu.org/cgit/stage0.git/tree/R EADME.org 🔲

[19]In theory, but we're not there yet. In 2020 Guix project came with 60 MB worth of binary stuff you have to trust. That's a big improvement over the 1+ GB Ubuntu download used by Gitian: https://guix.gnu.o rg/en/blog/2020/guix-further-reduces-bootstrap-seed-to-25/ 🔲

able to read some machine code that's typed by a human, or entered some other way, and then run that program.

The first program you feed it is an extremely simple compiler.[20] And once it has the rudimentary compiler, this new compiler reads another piece of source code, which then builds a slightly more complicated compiler. And then that slightly more complicated compiler builds another compiler. And this goes on for quite a while, until eventually, you have the modern C compiler that we all know and love, which is itself, of course, open source.

This compiler then builds a bunch of tools from source, ultimately producing a system very similar to Gitian — that is, a build system that avoids timestamps, doesn't use anything else from your computer, etc. In principle, it could build an entire operating system. So then your virtual machine or your physical machine would be running an operating system that you've built from scratch. But in this case, it just builds the compiler tools, and once those compiled tools are there, it can just start building Bitcoin Core as it would otherwise do.

This solves two things. First, it has no untrusted dependencies, so it's not using random libraries. And second, it's always using the same versions of libraries, which means that everybody can produce the same result.

Note that Guix doesn't solve the problem of dependencies entirely. It's a significant improvement over Gitian, but it's still critical to keep the number of dependencies small. Where Guix really shines is in mitigating the problem of trusting the build system.

---

[20]A compiler turns human-readable code into a binary that the computer can read. This implies that the first compiler is written in binary, which would have to be as small and well documented as possible.

Part IV

Better Wallets

Chapter 10

Script, P2SH, and Miniscript

Ep. 04

This chapter will talk about Miniscript and how it makes using Bitcoin Script much easier. It'll break down how Script works, how you can do more complicated and even absurd things with it, and how Miniscript emerged to make transactions less complicated and more secure. Additionally, it'll cover what policy language is and how it can make it easier to create scripts.

Constraints

Scripts are how the Bitcoin blockchain constrains how a given coin can be spent: When you want to receive bitcoin, you tell the person sending it what rules apply to the transaction. For example, with no constraints, anybody can touch whatever's in your wallet. Usually you would add the constraint that only you can spend these coins. Or, to be more precise, "These coins can only be spent if the transaction includes a signature that's made with a specific public key, i.e. my key."

So you'd tell the person sending bitcoin either your public key or the hash of it. This is what addresses are for, as we explained in chapter 1. Then, they'd put that on the blockchain with a note on it saying that only the owner of that public key can spend the bitcoin.

However, although this is by far the most common type of constraint, there are all sorts of other types of constraints, and you can even specify several different options for the spender, such as "I can spend this, but my mom also needs to sign it. But after two years, maybe I can sign it alone." In such a scenario, if you want to spend the money, you need to specify which option you're using and fulfill only the specific criteria for that option.

How Script Works

Script[1] is a stack-based language, so think of it like a stack of plates. You can put plates on it, and you can take the top plate off, but you can't manipulate plates in the middle.

A stack works differently than regular memory where you can read and write to arbitrary addresses (such as a hard disk or RAM — random-access memory). A stack is easier to implement and reason about.[2].

The most commonly used (before SegWit, see chapter 3) Bitcoin Script reads as follows:

- OP_DUP (as in duplicate)
- OP_HASH160 (which takes the SHA-256 hash twice, and then the RIPEMD-160 hash)
- pubKeyHash (the public key hash)

---

[1] https://en.bitcoin.it/wiki/Script

[2] In contrast, Ethereum smart contracts have a stack as well as regular memory and even longterm storage. As a consequence, it's much more difficult for developers to reason about its behavior. https://dlt-repo.net/storage-vs-memory-vs-stack-in-solidity-ethereum/

- OP_EQUAL_VERIFY
- OP_CHECKSIG

The value for pubKeyHash is generated by the recipient wallet by performing a double SHA-256 hash followed by RIPEMD-160, and the result is inserted into the above script. As explained in chapter 1, a Bitcoin *address* only contains the pubKeyHash; the rest is implied. It's actually the sender's wallet that generates the full script before publishing it on the blockchain.

On the blockchain this script ends up in the output of a transaction. The output of a transaction, i.e. a coin, consists of this script that it's locked with (scriptPubKey) and the amount. Now, if you want to spend that, you create a transaction input that instructs the blockchain to add certain things to the stack *before* the above script is executed.

The Bitcoin interpreter will see what you put on the stack, and it'll start running the program from the output. In this case, what you put on the stack is your signature and your public key, because the original script didn't have your public key; it had the hash of your public key.

Continuing with the example from above, we start with a stack that has two plates. The plate at the bottom is your signature, and on top of that is a plate with your public key, and then the script says OP_DUP. It pops the stack, i.e. it takes the top element from the stack — the top plate, which is the public key — and duplicates it. The original and duplicate are then pushed onto the stack. So now you have two plates with a public key at the top of the stack, and your signature's still at the bottom.

The next instruction is OP_HASH160. This pops one of those two duplicated public keys off the stack and hashes it, and then pushes that hash on the stack.

The signature is still at the bottom, and then there's a public key, and then there's the hash of the public key (three plates).

The next operation is **pubKeyHash**, which pushes the hash of your public key on the stack. So now, the hash of your public key occurs twice at the top of the stack.

The operation **OP_EQUAL_VERIFY** pops both these hashes of the stack and checks to see if they're the same.

What's left on the stack is your signature and your public key, so **OP_CHECKSIG** checks the signature using your public key, and then the stack is empty.

In a nutshell, that's how a Script program is run, and you can do arbitrarily complicated things along the way.

Script Hash and P2SH

In general, whenever you want to receive coins from someone, you have to specify exactly what script to use. In the above example, all that's needed is to provide the hash of the public key in a standardized address format, and the sender wallet creates the correct script.

But in the earlier more complicated example, with alternative conditions such as having a parent sign after a few years, communicating this becomes awkward. Even if there was an address standard, it would be a very long address indeed, due to all these different possible constraints.

Fortunately, there's an alternative to giving the counterparty (the sender) the full script — you can give them the hash of the script, which is always the same length, and also happens to be the same length as a normal address.

In 2012, the Pay-to-Script-Hash (P2SH) standard was introduced.[3] These kinds of transactions let you send to a script hash, which is an address beginning with 3, in stead of sending to a public key hash, which is an address beginning with 1.

---

[3]https://en.bitcoin.it/wiki/BIP_0016

The person on the other end has to copy-paste it, put it in their Bitcoin wallet, and send money to it. Now, when you want to spend that money, you need to reveal the actual script to the blockchain, which your wallet will handle automatically. Because all you need to share is a hash, the person that's sending you money doesn't need to care what this hash actually hides. Only when you spend the coins do you need to reveal the constraints. From a privacy point of view, this is much better than immediately putting the script on the chain. Chapter 11 will explain how Taproot takes this even further.

Similar to the workflow with regular P2PKH addresses, what you communicate to the sender is just the hash of the script. Before the sender's wallet puts that on the blockchain, it prepends OP_HASH160 and appends OP_EQUAL. So this is essentially a script within a script. The outer script, which the wallet puts on the blockchain, tells the blockchain there's an inner script that must be revealed *and satisfied* by the recipient in order to spend from it.

This last requirement does not actually follow from the script on the blockchain, which only requires the hash of the script to match. This is why the new P2SH address type came with a soft fork to enforce that when such a script within a script is found, it is also executed. This usually means that the spender doesn't just put the script on the stack, but also the ingredients necessary to satisfy the script, such as a signature.

Really Absurd Things

Script is a programming language that was introduced in Bitcoin, though it resembles a preexisting language known as Forth. It also seems to have been cobbled together as an afterthought. In fact, a lot of the operations that were part of the language were removed almost immediately, because there were all sorts of ways that you could just crash a node or do other bad things.[4]

The script's language is diverse enough to allow for weird stuff. If you just want somebody to send money to you, you only need this very simple standard script explained above: `OP_DUP OP_HASH160 <pubKeyHash> OP_EQUALVERIFY OP_CHECKSIG`.

But let's say you're collaborating, and you want to do a multi-signature, or multisig. To spend coins, two signatures need to provided, rather than just one. Now you could just use `OP_CHECKMULTISIG`, but let's say that didn't yet exist. Instead, you could take the script for one signature from above and more or less duplicate it, like so: `<KEY_A> OP_CHECKSIGVERIFY <KEY_B> OP_CHECKSIG`. In this example you're B, the second key that's checked (we also don't bother with hashing the public keys).

---

[4]Unfortunately, with Bitcoin, you can't just start with a draft language and then clean it up later. But this only became clear once developers realized the only safe way to upgrade Bitcoin is through very carefully crafted soft forks. Every change has to be backward compatible and not break any existing script. But developers can't always know the intention of scripts that are already out there, and worse still, as explained above, most scripts are hashed, so they could contain anything.

As a result, it's been a complete nightmare to make sure upgrades to the Script language don't do anything surprising or bad. If it turns out that existing nodes can be negatively impacted, e.g. crashed, by some obscure script, developers have to very carefully work around that issue; they have to fix the problem without accidentally making coins unspendable and without introducing new bugs, including in any unknown (hashed) script potentially out there.

Worse still, because Bitcoin is a live system and users can't be forced to all update at once, an ideal fix should not tip off an attacker as to what the issue is. But at the same time, it's an open source and transparent system, where changes can't go through without public justification. This makes Responsible Disclosure (https://github.com/bitcoin/bitco in/blob/master/SECURITY.md ▦) very complicated. So it's really best to go above and beyond to avoid such problems in first place.

Essentially, if you start with those two public keys and two signatures on the stack, and you run the script one instruction at a time, then if A and B put a valid signature on the stack, it's all good. This would be a poor man's multisig.

However, a malicious actor could insert an op code called OP_RETURN in the middle: <KEY_A> OP_CHECKSIGVERIFY OP_RETURN <KEY_B> OP_CHECKSIG.

This OP_RETURN code instructs the blockchain to stop evaluating the program — in other words, skipping the signature check for B, your signature.

If you naively looked at this script, you might think that your signature is checked at the end, and so the rest of the script isn't relevant. If you had a vigilant electronic lawyer (i.e. a person or computer program that does due diligence on transactions), who would properly check that this "smart contract" does what it says it does, they might say, "Careful there, your signature isn't getting checked." This hypothetical electronic lawyer should see that OP_RETURN "fine print" and warn you. But the problem is there are countless ways in which scripts can go wrong, which is why we need a standardized way of dealing with these scripts.

In an interview with Bitcoin Magazine,[5] Andrew Poelstra said, "There are opcodes in Bitcoin Script which do really absurd things, like, interpret a signature as a true/false value, branch on that; convert that boolean to a number and then index into the stack, and rearrange the stack based on that number. And the specific rules for how it does this are super nuts."

This quote exemplifies the complexity of potential ways to mess around with script.

To return to the plate analogy, you'd take a hammer and smash one, and then you'd confuse two and paint one

---

[5]https://bitcoinmagazine.com/technical/miniscript-how-blockstr eam-engineers-are-making-bitcoin-programming-easyer

red and then it would still work, if you do it correctly. It's completely absurd.

So that's the long[6] and short of the problem with scripts: It's easy to make mistakes or hide bugs and make all sorts of complex arrangements that people might or might not notice. And then your money goes places you don't want it to go. We've already seen in other projects, famously with the Ethereum DAO hack and resulting hard fork,[7] how bad things can get if you have a very complicated language that does things you're not completely expecting. But Bitcoin dodged many bullets in the early days, and despite its relative simplicity,[8] it still requires vigilance.

Enter Miniscript

Miniscript[9] is a project that was designed by a few Blockstream engineers: Pieter Wuille, Andrew Poelstra, and Sanket Kanjalkar. It's "a language for writing (a subset of) Bitcoin Scripts in a structured way, enabling analysis, composition, generic signing and more." You can see examples and try it yourself at http://bitcoin.sipa.be/miniscript ▓▓.

Miniscript consists of a few dozen script fragments, each a sequence of op codes. These fragments can be combined. If individual script op codes are like an alphabet then Miniscript fragments are like words. By building a script that only uses these words, rather than just any combination of letters from

---

[6]If you can't get enough of this, watch Andrew Poelstra's two-hour presentation at London Bitcoin Devs, where he goes on and on and on about the problems in script: https://www.youtube.com/watch?v=_v 1lECxNDiM ▓▓

[7]https://oguclturk.medium.com/the-dao-hack-explained-unfort unate-take-off-of-smart-contracts-2bd8c8db3562 ▓▓

[8]https://blockstream.com/2018/11/28/en-simplicity-github/ ▓▓

[9]https://medium.com/blockstream/miniscript-bitcoin-scripting-3aeff3853620 ▓▓

the alphabet, you lose some Script features, but you gain certain guarantees about safety and correct behavior.

A simple example of Miniscript is `pkh(A)` — which consists of only a single fragment. It's the equivalent of the standard P2PKH script analyzed above (`OP_DUP OP_HASH160 <pubKeyHashA> OP_EQUALVERIFY OP_CHECKSIG`). The poor man's multisig above requires several Miniscript fragments: `and_v(v:pk(pubKeyA),pk(pubKeyB))`.

Miniscript makes sure there's no funny stuff in the fine print. It removes some of the foot guns,[10] but it also allows you to do very cool stuff safely. In particular, it lets you do things like `AND`. So you can say condition `A` must be true `AND` condition `B` must be true, and you can do things like `OR`. And whatever's inside the `OR` or inside the `AND` can be arbitrarily complex.

In contrast, with Bitcoin Script, you have `if` and `else` statements, but if you're not careful, those `if` and `else` statements won't do what you think they're going to do, because there's complexity hidden after these statements.

Meanwhile, with Miniscript, the templates make sure you're only doing things that are actually doing what you think they're doing. Let's say you're a company and you offer a semi-custodial wallet solution, where you have one of the keys of the user and the user has the other has two keys. You don't have a majority of the keys, but maybe there's a five-year timeout where you do have control in case the user dies or something else happens.

This would be like a multisig set up. Normally, when you set up a multisig, everybody gives their public key[11] for example, and you create a simple script that has three keys

---

[10] An unsafe piece of code that causes users to shoot themselves in the foot. Early Bitcoin developer Gregory Maxwell was using this term as early as 2012, see e.g. https://github.com/bitcoin/bitcoin/pull/1889 #issuecomment-9638527 ▓, but it may be older

[11] Usually everyone would provide not just one public key, but a whole series of public keys, by using an extended public key, or xpub

and three people sign. But the problem is, because you're a big business that offers a service, you have some really complicated internal accounting department and you maybe want to have five different signatures by specific people with varied levels of complexity.

There's a lot of complex stuff you can do with it, and all the complex stuff should count as one key.

The problem with that is how does the customer know the script is OK? They'd have to hire their own electronic lawyer to check that the script doesn't have any little gimmicks in it.

Miniscript allows you to check that. A futuristic wallet could show you a little pie chart, saying "You're this one piece of the pie, and there's this other piece of the pie that's really complicated, but you don't have to worry about it. It's not going to do anything sneaky."

Policy Language

A policy language is a way to express your intentions. It's easier than writing a Miniscript directly, let alone writing Bitcoin Script directly. A compiler then does the hard work.

Our earlier example of a poor man's multisig was actually found this way. Starting with a policy `and(pk(KEY_A),pk(KEY_B))`, the compiler produced `and_v(v:pk(KEY_A),pk(KEY_B))`, which is equivalent to the script `<KEY_A> OP_CHECKSIGVERIFY <KEY_B> OP_CHECKSIG`. It turns out this actually produces a lower fee transaction than `<KEY_A> <KEY_B> 2 OP_CHECKMULTISIG`. This is the kind of optimization a human might overlook, which is what compilers are good for.

Basically, you write a policy language, which is like a higher-level programming language, which the compiler turns into low level op codes. These are instructions like the ones we described above for popping things off the stack and duplicating them. Miniscript also lives at that very low level, even if it's slightly more readable and a lot safer. It's the compiler's job to take a high level language like Policy Language and turn into the most efficient low-level code.

In the case of multisig, you might say, "I just want two out of two signatures. I don't care how you do that." The compiler knows there are multiple ways to execute the intention. And then, the question is, which of them will be picked? The answer to that depends on the transaction weight and the fees that might be involved.

However, you can also tell the compiler, "OK, I think most of the time it's condition A, but only 10 percent of the time it's condition B." The compiler would then calculate the fee for condition A, multiply by 9, add the fee for condition B and divide the total by 10 in order to get the average expected fee. It can optimize for typical use cases, worst case scenarios, all these things, and it then spits out a Miniscript which can then be transpiled to Bitcoin Script.[12]

With Taproot (see chapter 11), rather than splitting different conditions using *and / or*, they can be split into a Merkle tree of scripts. You don't have to worry about how to build the Merkle tree, as the compiler takes care of that. In principle, each leaf can also contain *and / or* statements. Does it make sense to do that? Or is it better to stick to one condition per leaf? Who knows? A future Miniscript compiler can just try all permutations and decide what's optimal.

---

[12]The technical term for going from Miniscript to Script — or for transforming source code from any language into another similar one — is transpiling, which can basically be done in two directions. So you can go from Miniscript to Script, or from Script to Miniscript, but you can't trivially go back to a policy language. However, using automated analysis tools, you can often still figure out what policy language was used to produce a given piece of Miniscript.

Limitations

All this said, there are some limitations when you're using policy language or Miniscript in general.

To ensure Miniscript and its corresponding Bitcoin Script can be safely reasoned about, it does not provide access to the full power of script. Sometimes, however, doing things safely results in a script that's unacceptably long and expensive to execute. In that case, a human may be able to construct a better solution. In regard to the example Poelstra mentioned in the context of how transactions for the Lightning network deal with time locks, hashes, or nonces, there are some optimizations. As he put it: "Oh, you do some weird switching of the stack and you interpret things, not the way they were." You put a public key on it, but you interpret it as a number — those kind of weird tricks.

Those might be very hard to reason about, and a human might be able to do it, but the Miniscript compiler wouldn't, which means the compiler would end up with potentially longer Lightning scripts. Perhaps one day Miniscript can be expanded so it can also find these shortcuts. But the Miniscript developers have to be careful, because they really want to make sure there's nothing in Miniscript that brings back the scary properties of the underlying language.

Another limitation is policy language is just one of several tools needed to make very complicated multisig wallets a practical reality. There are still questions left to answer, such as: How exactly do you do this setup? What are you emailing to each other? Are you emailing your keys or are you emailing something a little bit more abstract that you agree on first and then you exchange keys? These are practical things that aren't solved inside a Miniscript.

At the time of writing, integrating Miniscript into the Bitcoin Core wallet is still very much a work in progress.[13]

---

[13]https://github.com/bitcoin/bitcoin/pull/24149

Part V

Taproot

Overview

This part is all about Taproot: what it is, why it's interesting, and how it came to be.

Taproot is an upgrade to Bitcoin that was proposed in 2018 and deployed in November 2021. This soft fork increases privacy for "smart contracts" and reduces their transaction fees. It achieves this by hiding all the different spending conditions in a Merkle tree and only revealing the one that's eventually used. It also introduces Schnorr signatures, which make it much easier to compress signatures from multiple participants into a single signature. Both of these things result in less use of precious block space, reduced fees, and improved privacy.

Chapter 11 breaks down and explains Taproot[14] — covering the building blocks that make Taproot possible — and outlines what it enables Bitcoin to do.

Chapter 12 goes into how the Taproot soft fork was activated and the discussion that went into it.

---

[14]See also: https://bitcoinmagazine.com/articles/taproot-coming-what-it-and-how-it-will-benefit-bitcoin ▦

Chapter 11

Taproot and Schnorr

Ep. 02

In this chapter, we first introduce a Merkle tree that hides all the different spending conditions until they're used. This is called MAST. Next, we explain how Schnorr signatures allow us to hide the MAST itself, which improves privacy further. We cover earlier proposals for MAST, which didn't have the benefit of Schnorr, which in turn illustrates the power of Taproot. Finally, we point out some cool things Taproot enables.

Merklized Abstract Syntax Trees

Chapter 10 covered how the Pay-to-Script-Hash (P2SH) soft fork from 2012 made it possible to hide the contents of a script until it's spent. From a privacy point of view, this is much better than immediately putting the script on the chain. However, what's unfortunate about this is that when you do spend, all the constraints that were placed on the transaction are then visible to everyone.

The example from that chapter outlines a scenario where you need to either have your mom cosign a transaction or else wait two years to spend the coins on your own. One

potential downside of showing the contents of the entire
script, including the fallback condition, is that an attacker
learns that they only need to steal *your* keys and are then
free to spend the coins after two years. The very first time
you add coins to this particular wallet, the attacker won't
know anything about how to spend it (thanks to P2SH). And
if you only use that wallet once in your lifetime and spend all
of it at once, then the attacker won't learn about the fallback
until it's too late. However, if you use the wallet more than
once, then as soon as you make your first spend from it,
you'll have revealed that the fallback condition exists. From
then on, you're in trouble.

This scenario is exaggerated for educational purposes,
but the point stands: Once you spend money, it'd be nice
to only reveal the solution you use and not all the other
options.

This is where Merklized Abstract Syntax Trees (MAST[1])
come in.

A Merkle tree[2] is a tree of hashes of scripts, and it
specifies the different ways to spend Bitcoin. Picture it
upside down, with the root at the top and the leaves at the
bottom. So, if you have a list of four conditions, you build
up the tree by starting with those four conditions (or hashes)
at the bottom. Then, you bundle them into pairs, resulting
in two groups of hashes. They'd again be hashed, up and
up the tree, until there's one hash left at the top, the root,
which is the one you share: It's used to generate the address
where coins are sent to.

Later, when you want to spend it, you say, "This is the
part of the tree I want to spend," and then you use that
script. You also give the neighbor's script hash, because

---

[1] https://bitcoinops.org/en/topics/mast/
[2] Not to be confused with Merkel's tree: https://www.reddit.com/r
/ProgrammerHumor/comments/qzwjm3/please_dont_confuse_these
_two/

scripts come in pairs, and you give a hash of every other point in the tree. By revealing the script and its neighbor leaf hash, you prove you didn't change the script. This is called a Merkle proof, which we explained in more detail in chapter 6.

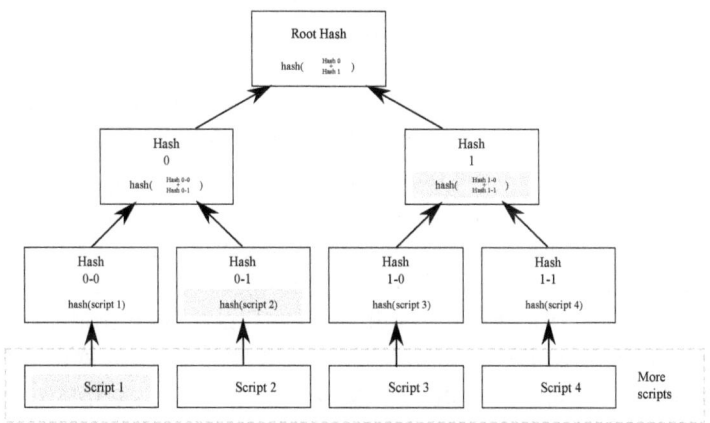

Merkle tree for MAST. To prove the existence of Script 1, you need to provide a Merkle proof consisting of the three marked items.

In this example with four conditions, the tree is three levels high. Since you already reveal the script, there's no need to reveal its hash. That leaves only two hashes to reveal: your script's neighbor leaf at bottom, and the neighbor of their parent (where the tree is two hashes wide). The top hash doesn't need to be revealed, because anyone can calculate it from the two hashes you provided. Depending on the scripts, this usually requires less data than the original four scripts, and you keep everything else secret. With 1,024 scripts, you only need to put the script you used, plus nine hashes, on the blockchain.

Now, Merkle trees are common: They're used in blocks, for file sharing, in BitTorrent, etc. Using them enables you to only share the parts of something you need. In the context

of Bitcoin, that might be the script you're using to spend
a coin, whereas in the context of BitTorrent, that might be
a specific two seconds of video; your computer can receive
lots of short fragments and confidently store those on your
hard disk, knowing it's really a piece of the movie you're
downloading, and not some garbage data. In both scenarios,
the rest remains hashed, and you just add some extra data
to prove that it — the script or a slice of the video file —
was in that tree somewhere.

In addition to keeping things secret, using MAST is also
less expensive, because you don't need to include all of the
possible scripts in the blockchain. This is especially true for
big trees with lots of scripts, which a "smart contract" might
need. The blockchain is a scarce resource, and including
everything costs a lot. When spending a coin, you have to
reveal the script, which requires fees. Since the introduction
of P2SH, it's the spender who reveals the script. Without
MAST, the spender has to reveal all possible scripts, but
with MAST, they only have to reveal the script that was
actually used.

Hiding the MAST

While Merkle trees are a good solution, it'd be even better if
you could hide the very MAST itself. Ideally, nobody even
knows you're using MAST.

Let's return to the previous example of you and your
mom. In this smart contract, if you and your mom both
agree to spend the money, you don't have to wait two years.
In most smart contracts, no matter how complicated the
various possible scripts are, when everyone who's involved
agrees to spend the money, they might as well dispense with
the scripts and just create a single joint signature.

It'd be nice to have a way to express this using only
the signature — without scripts or an entire tree. This can
be done by tweaking your public key, as discussed in BIP

341.[3] Instead of saying, "Send this to my public key," you'd instead say, "Send this to my public key, plus my mom's public key, plus this MAST key."

This tweaking of keys is slightly more complicated than literally adding them, owing to the many subtleties of cryptography, but in essence, if you can add up keys, and you can also add up signatures, and it looks to the outside world as if it's just a regular signature. As a result, you can hide things inside — but this process is extremely difficult without Schnorr.

Schnorr

Chapter 4 talks about libsecp256k1, and in May 2021, BIP 340[4] support was merged into libsecp256k1. This added Schnorr signatures to Bitcoin Core.

Schnorr digital signatures were first created by Claus-Peter Schnorr, a German mathematician. He created the Schnorr signature algorithm, which he then patented. It would've been great for Bitcoin, as well as many other open source projects that came before it, but because of the patent, people had to find another way to reap the benefits of these signatures.

So a bunch of lawyers, engineers, and cryptographers joined forces and tried to figure out if there was a way to maim Schnorr's algorithm so far that it would legally not fall under the patent, but still work. The result was a signature algorithm called Elliptic Curve Digital Signature Algorithm (ECDSA), which is the elliptic curve algorithm that Bitcoin currently uses and that the libsecp library implements. Although both Schnorr and ECSDA use public and private keys to create digital signatures, the latter involves a slightly more complicated process.

---

[3]Taproot (SegWit v1): https://en.bitcoin.it/wiki/BIP_0341
[4]Schnorr: https://en.bitcoin.it/wiki/BIP_0340

Although ECDSA is a convoluted version of Schnorr, it was standardized in 2005, and at least a dozen cryptographic libraries implemented it, including OpenSSL. And so, when Satoshi had to pick a cryptographic curve for Bitcoin, he chose ECDSA namely because it wasn't patented and it's already in OpenSSL.

Overall, Schnorr is simpler than ECDSA. They use the same elliptic curve, but to make a signature, you have to do slightly different calculations with it. So that also means that the change for Schnorr isn't as complicated as, say, the initial version of libsecp was.

The initial version of libsecp had to implement the elliptic curve, including all the operations you can do in a curve, like addition and multiplication, and then implement the signature algorithm of ECDSA. But for Schnorr, you just need to do the signature algorithm for Schnorr, and you can skip — or remove — all the needless math.

Moving from ECDSA to Schnorr isn't a huge change; it's not modifying the elliptic curve or introducing an entirely new one. Rather, it's a different — and simpler — way of signing.

The fewer changes developers have to make to a cryptographic library, the better. It means fewer places where critical bugs can be introduced. It also means less code review for the community. With almost a trillion dollars at stake, any bug related to Bitcoin's digital signatures could have disastrous consequences, so the importance of only needing a simple change is difficult to overstate.

On top of that, because Schnorr is added as a soft fork, using it is entirely opt-in. ECDSA isn't going anywhere.

But Why Schnorr?

Simplicity is great, but all the hard work for the more complicated ECDSA had already been done. Why bother changing things? Even before Taproot, people wanted to add Schnorr because of all the things it enabled. But at some point, Bitcoin Core contributor and former Blockstream CTO Gregory Maxwell came up with a clever way of using Schnorr in combination with MAST.

Basically, because you can add anything to a public key, you can also add a script to a public key, because a script is essentially just a number and a private key is essentially just a number, and numbers can be added. Converting an elliptic curve private key to a public key also happens to be commutative. That let's you do this:

```
public_key(private key + hash) ==
public_key(private_key) + public_key(hash)
```

Let's now use an example of a backup system that you'd need in case you forget your private key. You start out with two keys: a primary key and a backup key. You keep your primary key on a very secure and tamperproof hardware wallet at home. Your backup key could be a note in a remote safe. If your house burns down, or if the hardware bricked itself after three incorrect PIN attempts, or if it's stolen, you effectively lose the primary private key. So you'd fetch your backup key.

The backup key is what goes *in* the MAST. If you never use it, nothing on the blockchain will indicate that you even have this backup. Under normal circumstances, you'd only use the primary key without revealing the MAST or the backup key in it.

But how does this hiding of the MAST work? Well that's where Schnorr comes in. Schnorr lets you take this MAST and hide it inside your public key. Your wallet adds the root hash of the MAST to your private key, and then it calculates the corresponding, tweaked, public key. That tweaked key is what you put on the blockchain. To the outside world, it looks like any old public key.

And then, when you sign an actual transaction, you sign for this tweaked public key. Anyone else doesn't see any difference between a tweaked public key and one that isn't tweaked; they're both perfectly valid public keys. Again, whether or not you tweaked your public key with this MAST structure, it looks the same to the rest of the world.

Only when you need to use your backup key is it time to reveal the MAST structure. Instead of using the tweaked key in your transaction, you reveal the original untweaked key, and you reveal the script (or one of your scripts, if you have a more complicated setup with more scripts in the tree).

Then, any person verifying, i.e. everyone who runs a full node, will take that script, calculate the hash, and add it up to the public key. They'll see that this matches the tweaked key that was already on the blockchain, which proves you didn't just make up a new script. The new script reveals to the world what your backup public key is, and they'll check if your signature was indeed made using the private key for that public key.

Using this approach of a public key tweaked with a MAST is very space efficient. It improves privacy overall, because there's no difference between transactions that pay to an individual with a simple single-key wallet and those that pay to an exchange with a super fancy multi-signature setup. It all looks the same, unless any of the backup conditions are used.

In the earlier example of you and your mom, if you accept Bitcoin with your mom this way, the first step is for the two of you to combine your public keys.[5] Next, you generate a

---

[5]The art of combining public keys and making joint signatures deserves a chapter of its own. It's an important feature that Schnorr enables. But Taproot doesn't do this for you. That's up to wallet software and this is still a work in progress. The MuSig2 protocol is the latest proposal for how future wallet software can do this in a provably secure manner: https://eprint.iacr.org/2020/1261

MAST with at least one leaf: the script specifying that after two years, you can spend the coins alone.[6]

Under normal circumstances, when you want to spend some coins, you call your mom and produce a joint signature. The coin you spend from specifies the public key, which has been tweaked with the MAST Merkle root. So you tweak your private key before producing a signature with it. What you publish will look like a regular signature for everyone else (because it is).

However, if there's a scenario where one of you can't sign and those two years go by, at the end you can reveal that it was actually a tweaked public key.[7] The rest of the world can look at that and say, "Yep. That adds up. The math makes total sense. That was what you were always doing; we just never were able to see it. Yep, two years have passed, so you're allowed to spend this money now on your own."

As a result, the condition is only revealed if you actually use it. Otherwise, it'll be a secret forever, unless somebody hacks your wallet.

The ability to have multiple conditions and only reveal one of those conditions is what MAST enables. The ability to combine public keys with other keys and hashes is what Schnorr enables.[8]. But, this magic is combined, like Captain Planet, and now you can hide the MAST.

---

[6]It might also contain a second leaf that allows you and your mom to bypass the MuSig2 protocol and instead provide two individual signatures. This isn't as good in terms of privacy, and it incurs higher fees, but it's easier in some circumstances.

[7]Under the hood, every Taproot spend involves a tweaked key, using an empty MAST if there are no script leafs.

[8]https://bitcoinmagazine.com/articles/the-power-of-schnorr-the-signature-algorithm-to-increase-bitcoin-s-scale-and-privacy-1460642496

Earlier MASTs

To appreciate Taproot even more, let's take a brief excursion back in time.

The first MAST proposal, BIP 114,[9] introduced a new SegWit version. It offered privacy benefits similar to the Taproot Merkle tree proposal, and it only revealed the spending condition or script that was used.

Instead of introducing a new SegWit version, the second MAST proposal, BIP 116,[10] added a new opcode, `MERKLEBRANCHVERIFY`, to the existing script system. While the privacy was the same, the implementation varied.

However, there are downsides to both of these earlier MAST proposals:

1. As soon as you spend it, everyone can see that a MAST tree existed, even if they can't see the full contents of the tree.
2. In the case where everyone agrees, you can't just ignore the script and put signatures on the chain: You still have to pick a "we all agree" script from the MAST tree and satisfy it, which uses precious blockchain bytes.

By tapping the MAST root onto a Schnorr public key, so to speak, you fix these issues, as explained above.

But Wait, There's More. . .

While it's true that some of the things you can do with Taproot were already technically possible (but more complicated), there are also some things Taproot unlocks.

For example, M-of-N signatures, or multi signatures, can now be done without a script, because Taproot enables

---

[9]MAST: https://en.bitcoin.it/wiki/BIP_0114 🔳

[10]`MERKLEBRANCHVERIFY`: https://en.bitcoin.it/wiki/BIP_0116 🔳

protocols for combining them. This was possible before with threshold signatures in ECDSA,[11] but like everything before Schnorr, it was complicated, and now it's slightly easier.

To the outside world, a threshold signature looks like a single public key and a single signature. For M-of-M signatures, e.g. 2-of-2, the MuSig2 algorithm can be used. For the more general M-of-N, there's no recommended algorithm yet. This isn't a problem, because the algorithm for combining keys and signatures doesn't need to be baked into the protocol; the Bitcoin protocol just needs to support Schnorr. When someone comes up with a new way to combine signatures, the result will look like a single signature — not just to humans, but also to nodes. And single signatures can be verified.

Another cool feature is how Taproot can make the Lightning network,[12] which is a layer 2 payment protocol, more private. Payments on Lightning involve passing a hash around, which is the same for all intermediate hops. This is a potential privacy concern, because someone with access to many nodes on the network could reconstruct the route a given payment took. With Schnorr, these hashes can be replaced with elliptic curve points that are different for each hop.[13]

Additionally, Lightning uses channels, which are coins protected by two signatures, and with Taproot:

1. Those two signatures can be combined into one signature (e.g. using MuSig2).
2. The scripts Lightning uses to enforce good behavior can be hidden in the MAST, only to be revealed in the case of misbehavior.

---

[11]https://eprint.iacr.org/2020/1390.pdf
[12]https://lightning.network/
[13]https://bitcoinops.org/en/topics/ptlc/

In other words, if both sides of the channel agree on an operation, it looks like a normal transaction to outsiders. But if they disagree, there are a lot of additional timeout conditions, which can be nicely hidden inside the MAST.

However, most people won't necessarily notice much of a difference, except that privacy will be slightly better. As these advanced options come along, they'll use them but not notice them. That said, taking advantage of this functionality makes things cheaper, easier, and more private.

Chapter 12

Activation Options

Ep. 03

The Taproot soft fork was activated on November 13, 2021, approximately one year after the finalized code was merged.[1] It happened much more quickly than SegWit did, and with far less drama, but it wasn't an uneventful year. This chapter discusses how soft forks were activated in the past, what options were considered for Taproot, and how Taproot was finally activated.

We dedicated five episodes to this topic, and the QR codes are placed at various points in this chapter. However, it's far from a one-to-one mapping; they're not even in chronological order.

Soft Forks: A Primer

As Taproot's deployment grew close, the question of how to activate soft forks once again became a topic of debate in the Bitcoin community.

Soft forks, if you recall, are changes to the protocol that are backward compatible. In other words, anyone who has

---

[1]https://github.com/bitcoin/bitcoin/pull/19953

upgraded will reap the benefits of new changes, but those who don't upgrade will still find their software working.

In addition to introducing new features, a soft fork can be used to get rid of bugs and potential vulnerabilities — at least, some of them. The way this is done is by making the rules stricter, but without suddenly freezing anybody's coins.

A simple example of such stricter rules is BIP 66,[2] which mandated that any new signatures had to conform to a strict standard, whereas there was previously some (unintended) flexibility in how to encode signatures.[3]

It may seem paradoxical that strict rules allow for *more* features, but in chapter 3, under the future SegWit versions section, we explained why this works. In this chapter, we're less concerned with how soft forks work, and instead we focus on how they're activated.

There are a few different ways to introduce a soft fork. You can do it randomly by accident, or you can deliberately sneak one into the code. You can also announce a date (known as a flag day) or block height from which the new rules apply. Finally — and this is how things currently work — you can have miners signal and have the soft fork activate once a certain threshold is reached.

But perhaps what matters more than the mechanics of activation is how a decision is reached to deploy the soft fork in the first place. And who decides anyway?

The Earliest Soft Forks

Although the term didn't yet exist in the early days, there were many soft forks, mostly related to closing security holes

---

[2]https://en.bitcoin.it/wiki/BIP_0066

[3]https://technicaldifficulties.io/2020/07/22/bip-66-unpacking-der-signatures/

in the early prototype.[4] In 2013, there was even an accidental soft fork, and in 2015, there was a near-miss accidental soft fork due to OpenSSL changes (see chapter 4).

The earliest soft forks mostly used a block height as their method of activation — in other words, "as of this future block, the new rule shall apply." Ideally this is announced well in advance, giving people plenty of time to upgrade. For a "secret" soft fork, developers might simply insist that people upgrade and then explain the reason afterward.

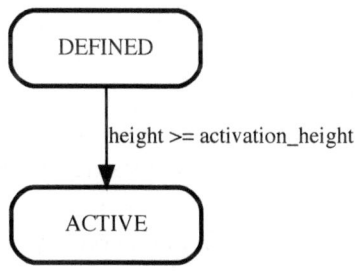

Informal diagram of a flag height-activated soft fork

Probably the most infamous soft fork of all time is the one-megabyte block size limit introduced by Satoshi in 2010.[5]

---

[4]https://blog.bitmex.com/bitcoins-consensus-forks/

[5]Since the very first release of version 0.1.0 on January 9, 2009, there has been a 32MB limit (`MAX_SIZE`) that applies to various things. This includes the block size, which was checked in `CheckBlock()`. See https://satoshi.nakamotoinstitute.org/code/. Then, on July 15, 2010, Satoshi introduced `MAX_BLOCK_SIZE=1000000` and changed the miner software to not produce blocks larger than that in https://github.com/bitcoin/bitcoin/commit/a30b56ebe76ffff9f9cc8a6667186179413c6349. So far, no soft fork. It was just a change to the software used by miners, which they could've reverted without producing invalid blocks. Months later, on September 7, he modified a related function, `AcceptBlock()`, to enforce `MAX_BLOCK_SIZE` https://github.com/bitcoin/bitcoin/commit/f1e1fb4bdef878c8fc1564fa418d44e7541a7e83. This was the actual soft fork, and it was released the same day in v0.3.12. Both commits pretended to do completely unrelated things. Nowadays, code reviewers frown upon commits that touch anything outside the area they claim to change — even if just removing a blank line.

The soft fork was released on September 7, 2010, and its `activation_height` was set to 79,400, which occurred just a week later.[6].

Not only was Satoshi's decision to impose this limit a unilateral one, but he did it secretly. He probably found it safer to keep this change under wraps because he didn't want to alert potential attackers to a gaping security hole, wherein massive blocks could have ground the network to a halt.[7]

It's not that nobody looked at the source code changes, because in the forum where Satoshi announced this new release, there was discussion of *another* soft fork at that same height. In any case, nobody paid much attention to it until many years later, when this reduced limit became a practical issue in the form of increasing fees for scarce block space.

But barring some existential emergency, there's a general consensus that this isn't an acceptable way of introducing a soft fork now. If there had been a debate on the block size limit back then, perhaps the drama that came later could've been prevented.

How Is a Soft Fork Enforced?

Releasing a new software version that activates a soft fork at a given height is one thing. But unless the right people

---

[6]https://bitcointalk.org/index.php?topic=999.msg12181 ▦

[7]Back in 2017, I ran an experiment where I took older versions of Bitcoin Core and measured how long it took them to catch up to the present-day blockchain. Modern nodes did this many times faster, thanks to various improvements over the years (see e.g. chapter 5). But more importantly, Bitcoin Core v0.5, released in 2012, was completely unable to keep up with the chain. It would just crash or grind to a halt for weeks. Without the block size limit introduced by Satoshi, anyone back in 2012 could've produced huge blocks that then would've overwhelmed the available node software (see appendix A).

run it and do so in time, it won't actually take effect. If a soft fork is released in a forest...

What Satoshi did was announce the new version on a forum and presume the community was small enough that everyone would update well before the activation height, even if that was only a week away. This was generally not put to the test, because many of those initial soft forks were made in such a way, either by design or accident, that only a malicious actor would produce blocks that violate the new rule, and there weren't many of them around.

Despite that, even in 2010, there was a growing understanding that the safest way to enforce a soft fork is to have a supermajority of miners run the latest version. This is because nodes will follow the longest chain that they consider valid. So even if a user hasn't upgraded their node, as long as the majority of miners are enforcing the rules, they'll produce the longest chain, and the user's node will follow along. This way, even if a miner maliciously or accidentally produces an invalid block, the majority of miners won't build on top of it, and the invalid block goes stale.[8]

We don't know how many individual miners there were in 2010, but it's conceivable they were very much on top of these updates.[9] And there wasn't any money to be made from mining: The first pizza sale was only in May of that year.[10] Even in 2013, when an accidental soft fork happened, enough miners deployed the fix in just a few hours.[11] But emergencies aren't the same as regular soft forks.

---

[8]See chapter 7 for an explanation of stale blocks.

[9]Some speculate that a single miner nicknamed Patoshi, not necessarily Satoshi, controlled more than 50 percent of the hash rate until February 2010: https://whale-alert.medium.com/the-satoshi-fortune-e49cf73f9a9b

[10]https://bitcoinmagazine.com/culture/the-man-behind-bitcoin-pizza-day-is-more-than-a-meme-hes-a-mining-pioneer

[11]https://bitcoinmagazine.com/technical/bitcoin-network-shaken-by-blockchain-fork-1363144448

Who Decides?

Initially, Satoshi would unilaterally decide what to change, though he ultimately couldn't force anyone to run the new versions he released, so he couldn't make completely arbitrary controversial changes.[12] Nowadays, without going too deep in the weeds, Bitcoin development follows a process of "rough consensus," as described in RFC 7282.[13]

Anyone can propose a change to the rules of Bitcoin. But they not only need to convince others of the usefulness; they also need to address all technical objections that are raised to it. For example, if someone complains that a proposal would break their (wallet) software, the proposal author can't simply say "tough luck." Instead, they have to address the issue. Maybe they can propose a simple fix for the wallet in question, or they can modify their own proposal so it doesn't break stuff.

This — along with a few other requirements — usually involves a lot of back and forth on technical mailing lists, as well as many iterations of improving the proposal. Many proposals don't survive this process at all, because it turns out they cause too many problems.

Hard fork proposals often get rejected based on just the fact that they both break existing software and require every participant to upgrade at the same time. A soft fork variant of the same proposal would address both concerns, so it's generally preferred instead. This is why Bitcoin Core developer Luke Dashjr's offhand suggestion that SegWit could be

---

[12]It's best to leave the party while you're still having fun, and perhaps he did just that: "But as frustrations with his authority and availability built, it became all too common for users to decry Satoshi the admin, Satoshi the bottleneck, Satoshi the dictator." https://bitcoinmagazine.com/technical/what-happened-when-bitcoin-creator-satoshi-nakamoto-disappeared

[13]https://datatracker.ietf.org/doc/html/rfc7282

implemented as a soft fork was such a game changer.[14]

In addition to not having any unaddressed objections, there's also the need to get enough experienced developers to review a proposal. Lack of enthusiasm among a very small group of such experienced developers can cause a perfectly fine soft fork to never see the light of day. Or, more often, a lack of reviewer enthusiasm combined with difficult-to-address technical problems will keep the proposal in limbo.

But if all goes well and the code ends up merged into the Bitcoin Core software, there's still the matter of what activation procedure to apply. This is subject to the same kind of rough consensus discussion as a proposal; people may love a proposed soft fork but object to a flag day activation for all the reasons explained above. To avoid scenarios where proposals get stuck in a discussion about their activation, ideally the community agrees on a single activation mechanism that's applied for every soft fork. But, well, that turns out to be a challenge.

Signaling (BIP 9)

So if a flag day or block height isn't the best way to activate soft forks, how can we do better? One idea was to have miners signal readiness in the blocks they create. Initially, this was done by increasing the block version number.[15] Signaling works as a coordination mechanism for the network to figure out that enough miners have upgraded.

The mechanism was improved and further formalized in BIP 9.[16] As part of the signaling mechanism embedded in the code, there's a starting date (**starttime**) when miners begin

---

[14]https://news.ycombinator.com/item?id=11230394 ▨

[15]BIP 34 https://en.bitcoin.it/wiki/BIP_0034 ▨ in 2012 used version 2, and BIP 66 in 2015 used version 3. Once 95 percent of recent blocks contained this new version, the new rules would apply.

[16]https://en.bitcoin.it/wiki/BIP_0009 ▨

signaling, and a deadline (`timeout`) at which point they give up if the `threshold` wasn't reached. Tallying happens in rounds of 2,016 blocks, or about two weeks. If the threshold is reached in any round that ends before `timeout`, the new rules are active. This is easy for every node in the network to verify.

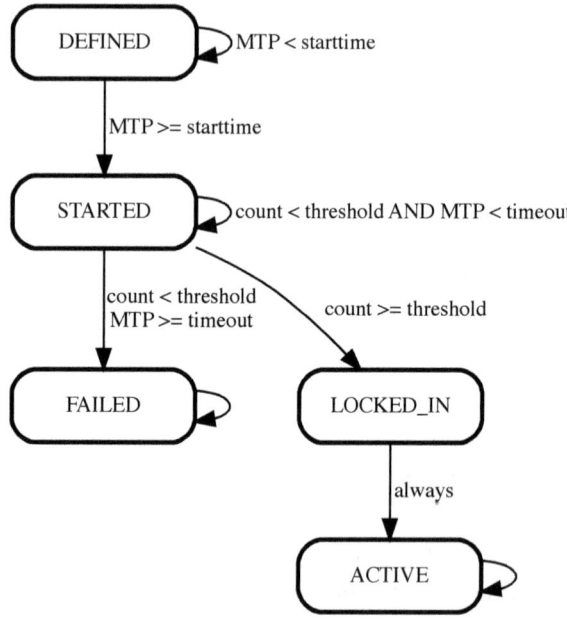

BIP 9 flow

The significance of 2,016 is that it's the number of blocks in a single difficulty adjustment period, or retarget period.[17] In the diagram above, each arrow represents one signaling period. The looping arrows indicate when the state stays the same — for example, when a soft fork is `DEFINED` (meaning the node knows about it, but there's no signaling yet), it'll stay that way if the MTP[18] is still below `starttime`. When it's at or after `starttime`, the state jumps to `STARTED`. It

---

[17]https://en.bitcoin.it/wiki/Difficulty

[18]MTP stands for Median Time Past, and it refers to the middle

stays there pending signaling. For each period — say every two weeks — we check if enough blocks are signaling. If so, we move to the next phase, which is LOCKED_IN. If not, and if timeout is reached, we move to FAILED. LOCKED_IN is a grace period where the new rules don't yet apply, but after two weeks, the soft fork is ACTIVE and the rules do apply.

Signaling hands control of upgrade activation to miners for a predefined period. It requires a signaling readiness of 95 percent for a soft fork activation to succeed.

This mechanism has the additional benefit of allowing the deployment of multiple soft forks in parallel. Each gets assigned a specific signaling bit.

BIP 9 was used successfully to deploy the CSV and SegWit soft forks, and it could've been used for Taproot as well. The first deployment went smoothly, but as we'll soon see, the second one involved much drama and took far longer than many people considered necessary. This led to worries that perhaps BIP 9 isn't a future-proof deployment mechanism.[19] As a result, several other mechanisms were proposed, along with variations on those mechanisms.

Always Verify Blocks!

Unfortunately, no amount of signaling is useful when miners don't actually enforce the new rules. Remember that we need the majority of miners, i.e. the longest chain, to enforce the new rules to protect non-upgraded nodes (which in turn allows these upgrades to remain non-mandatory).

During the BIP 66 soft fork in 2015, it turned out that a large portion of miners, despite signaling readiness, weren't

---

block of the last 11 blocks. This is a mechanism used to discourage miners from gaming the timestamp in each block.

[19]Its use of timestamps rather than block heights also seemed to needlessly complicate things.

verifying the new rules.[20] As soon a transaction that violated the new rules appeared in a block, those miners failed to reject it and instead kept building on top of it.[21] At the same time, the miners that upgraded and checked the new rules did reject the block. They produced an alternative, valid block at the same height and kept building on top of that new branch. Eventually, their new branch overtook the invalid branch, causing the non-verifying miners to switch over to the valid branch. The first time, the invalid chain branched off for six blocks. The next day, it happened again, but only for three blocks, perhaps because more miners upgraded their software as they became aware of the problem.

Skipping block verification is risky for miners even without a soft fork,[22] but under normal and benevolent circumstances, they may get away with it. However, in a soft fork where a majority of miners enforces the new rules, but a minority doesn't, when one of these minority miners accidentally mines an invalid block, other such non-verifying miners will build on top of it. The upgraded majority will ignore all these blocks, and once their chain is longer, all these minority miners find their blocks stale. That's what happened with BIP 66.

The First Drama, and BIP 148/91

When it was time to deploy SegWit, after the code was ready, BIP 9 was used again because it worked fine before. But as months went by, in none of the biweekly retargeting periods was the required 95 percent block signaling threshold

---

[20]https://www.reddit.com/r/Buttcoin/comments/6dvkr6/short_w riteup_of_the_bip66_disaster_is_this/

[21]https://bitcoin.org/en/alert/2015-07-04-spv-mining#cause

[22]It's even more reckless for miners to not even verify the *transactions* they selected to put in their own blocks. But back in 2015, there was at least one small miner who did this: https://www.reddit.com/r/Bit coin/comments/3c305f/comment/csrt3dg/

reached. Although one can't tell by looking at the blockchain, it appeared that several large miners were using the BIP 9 readiness signal, or lack thereof, as a vote, in turn blocking the upgrade.

They weren't raising any technical objections, so the previously established RFC 7282-style rough consensus was still intact. Was it just inertia and apathy? Was there a secret technical objection they had to the proposal?[23] Or were miners frustrated with and lacking confidence in the developers, perhaps in part due to language and cultural barriers?[24]

In any case, BIP 9 wasn't supposed to be a referendum, and given how quickly miners were able to upgrade with previous soft forks, this stalemate made little sense and frustrated those who wanted to take advantage of the SegWit features we discussed in chapter 3. One particularly frustrating aspect of this situation is that the lack of signaling was holding back the much demanded block size increase that SegWit offered.

At this point, most of the Bitcoin Core developers were perhaps just as frustrated, but they preferred to stay on the conservative side and simply wait for the `timeout` and some earlier success. When there's no consensus on a new course of action, the default is to just do nothing. But that doesn't have to stop anyone else.

Around early March of 2017, there was a group of people that said, "Hey, you know what? It's time for a flag day." They picked August 1, 2017, as a date and said that on that day, their nodes would enforce the new SegWit rules.

---

[23]It was speculated that a technique called covert AsicBoost was giving certain miners an advantage over their competitors that they preferred not to disclose: https://blog.bitmex.com/the-blocksize-war-chapter-14-asicboost/ ▨▨

[24]Many miners were Chinese, and many developers were from Western countries.

To be more precise, on that date, they would require all
blocks to signal for SegWit. That signaling would in turn
cause SegWit to activate. BIP 148 was the mechanism, and
it was commonly referred to as a User-Activated Soft Fork
(UASF).[25] The similarity of this acronym to a certain branch
of the US military was helpful in its marketing.

The question is: Did it work? One can't tell by just
looking at the blockchain. When you look at historical
blocks, you just see 95 percent signaled, and the soft fork
was activated. Now, it's of course very remarkable that
this activation occurred right before August 1 and not some
random other date that it could have happened. But there
are no stale branches of non-signaling blocks that we could
point to as evidence for a fight between miners and UASF
nodes.

As we'll explain in the `LOT=true` discussion below, it's
probably a good thing that no confrontation in the form of
competing blockchain branches happened.

A few days after BIP 148 was published, an alternative
to it was posted on the developer mailing list. It proposed
activating SegWit, along with an additional doubling of
the block size using a hard fork. We already pointed out
above that, thus far, hard fork proposals haven't survived
the technical objections raised against them, e.g. the need
for all node users and wallet software to upgrade at the same
time, and the mandatory nature of such an upgrade.

But despite not being well received in a technical forum,
a group of major companies in the space met in a New York
hotel and announced the so-called New York Agreement.[26]
They also added a lower activation signal threshold.

The Blocksize War (the book mentioned at the end of
chapter 3) goes into more detail about where all that led

---

[25]https://en.bitcoin.it/wiki/BIP_0148

[26]https://dcgco.medium.com/bitcoin-scaling-agreement-at-consen
sus-2017-133521fe9a77

(spoiler: They called off the hard fork at the last minute). For the purpose of this chapter, it's interesting to briefly explain the idea of lowering the activation threshold, which enjoyed a more positive reception.

The next day, BIP 91 was proposed on the mailing list.[27]. It worked as follows: If 80 percent of miners signaled in favor, then (two weeks later) all miners would need to signal. And once all miners signaled, the 95 percent threshold would be reached. This would cause SegWit to activate from the perspective of everyone involved.

Users that run the more conservative Bitcoin Core node would see the 95 percent signal and consider SegWit active. Users that run the more aggressive UASF node would see the same, provided it happened before August 1.

Similar to the situation with UASF, we can't really tell what happened by just looking at blocks.[28]

So in the end, all we can say is it didn't go wrong. Nobody called each other's bluff. But what did come out of it is that everyone realized it was important to rethink how to actually activate soft forks. Having a situation where miners block activation without (publicly sharing) a good technical reason isn't ideal. A bunch of contentious chain splits as different camps battle it out isn't great either — it defeats

---

[27]https://lists.linuxfoundation.org/pipermail/bitcoin-dev/2017-May/014380.html ▦

[28]SegWit signaled on bit 1, and the New York Agreement folks signaled on bit 4 (as did BIP 91). The bit 4 signal did cross the required threshold: https://bitcoinmagazine.com/technical/bip-91-has-activated-heres-what-means-and-what-it-does-not ▦. However, that doesn't prove that BIP 91 *caused* SegWit to activate. That's because things happened too quickly. During the retarget period, the BIP 91 status was `LOCKED_IN`, meaning it wasn't yet enforcing its 100 percent signaling requirement. But right in that period, SegWit reached its 95 percent threshold on bit 1. So in the next period, BIP 91 was `ACTIVE` and SegWit was `LOCKED_IN`. Both required 100 percent signaling at that point. In reality, it's likely that miners were simply setting bit 4, but not actually running any of the software that used it.

the purpose of carefully engineering soft forks that maintain
a well-functioning blockchain.

Rethinking Activation, and the Introduction of BIP 8

Inspired by UASF, as well seeing the need to clean up BIP
9, BIP 8[29] was proposed.[30] It uses a signaling mechanism
similar to BIP 9, but based on block height rather than
timestamps. This makes it easier to reason about reorgani-
zations, e.g. when the last block of a signaling period arrives
just *before* the `timeout`, a soft fork would activate, but then
if an alternate branch of blocks appears and takes over, and
this alternate branch arrives (has timestamps of) directly
after `timeout`, then — on that branch, that rewriting of
history — it wouldn't activate.

The downside of using a block height is that you can't pre-
dict on which date the `timeout` is going to happen, because
it depends on how fast blocks are produced.[31]

So far, BIP 8 would just be a nice drop-in replacement
for BIP 9. But where it really differentiates itself is in the
UASF-style flag date for forced signaling. This is indicated

---

[29]https://en.bitcoin.it/wiki/BIP_0008 ▣

[30]In case you're wondering why a new proposal gets a lower BIP
number, my guess is as follows: BIP numbers tend to be thematically
grouped in ranges of 10, e.g. BIP 340–343 all relate to Taproot. BIP
1 and 2 are meta issues, and they explain, among other things, how
Bitcoin ought to be upgraded. So it makes sense to include soft fork
activation logic in the single-digit range, but fill it out in descending
order.

[31]This is mainly a problem for developers who use the testnet to
test e.g. wallet software ahead of the real activation. On the testnet,
blocks don't arrive in semi-regular 10-minute intervals, but can instead
arrive in huge numbers. This makes it impossible to pick reasonable
activation heights. For a more thorough explanation and solution, see
appendix A for the episode about Signet.

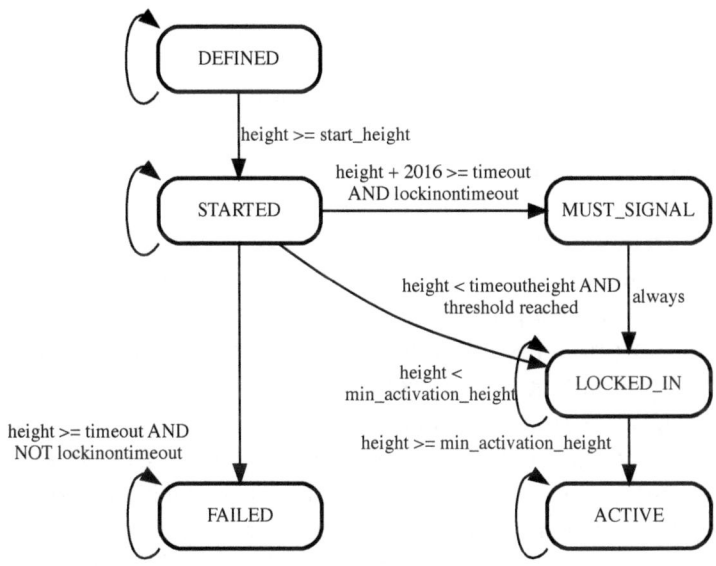

BIP 8 flow

by the MUST_SIGNAL phase in the diagram, which otherwise doesn't differ much from what you saw above with BIP 9.

What this means is that the flag date doesn't activate the soft fork itself. Rather, if, closer to the date, there's a block that isn't signaling support for the soft fork, that block will be rejected: That's how it forces signaling toward the end.

Like with the UASF, this forced signaling only makes sense if there are *other* nodes out there that don't have such a flag date.[32] This is why the flag day setting itself is optional. What exactly does optional mean here? It could mean that there are two different downloads: one with the flag day enabled and one without, presumably released by two separate teams with different priorities. It could also

---

[32]For nodes without that setting, the horizontal line from STARTED to MUST_SIGNAL is never used, and instead the vertical line from STARTED to FAILED would occur, and it's essentially BIP 9.

mean that there's a single download that allows the user to choose.

This allows for an escalation ladder: Perhaps most of the community starts out not using a flag date, and then as time goes by, more do.

In this sense, it formalizes the process that happened informally in 2017, basically saying: If you want to do something like a UASF, please do it in this specific way.

Just like its predecessor, UASF, this proposal isn't without its problems. The following paragraphs outline how forced signaling is supposed to work.

If you run a node with this feature enabled, then when, after the flag day, a block that doesn't include a signal is produced, your node will consider this block invalid, no matter how many other blocks are built on top of it. If some miners produce an alternative branch of blocks, even if it's shorter, that do include the signal, your node will follow that alternative branch. Eventually, if and only if enough blocks are produced on this alternative branch, the soft fork is guaranteed to activate.

On the other hand, *if you run a node without this feature*, or for that matter, if you run older node software that doesn't know about the soft fork, then you'll continue to follow the longest chain, regardless of what its block signal is. If the longest chain happens to comply with mandatory signaling, your node will follow it. If it doesn't comply, your node will also follow it. The scenario to worry about here is when, initially, the longest chain doesn't signal, but after some time it gets overtaken by a chain that does. Since your node doesn't care if blocks signal or not, it'll happily switch over to this new branch.

In any scenario where two alternative chains exist, it's unsafe for users whose node follows one branch to transact with users whose node follows the other branch. In fact, it's unsafe for *anyone* to use the blockchain at that point. On the other hand, as long as the only chain in existence complies with mandatory signaling, there's nothing to worry about. This might remind some readers of the game theory around mutual assured destruction (MAD).

To Argue a LOT

This setting to require mandatory signaling became known as LOT. We dedicated several episodes to the debate around it, not all of which made into this book. The transcript for the accompanying episode can be found here.[33]

Ep. 29   When it came to the Taproot activation process, there was a debate surrounding this LOT parameter, which stands for Lock-in On Timeout. If you refer to the BIP 8 diagram above, lockinontimeout appears in the horizontal arrow. When set to false we transition to FAILED after the soft fork times out. But when it's set to true, then in the very last 2,106-block retargeting period, we go to MUST_SIGNAL, and that's always followed by LOCKED_IN. In other words, we lock in right before ("on") the timeout, hence the name.

In other words, in the case of both LOT=false and LOT=true, miners can signal for an upgrade for one year. Then, if the specified threshold percentage — in the case of Taproot, 90 percent — is met, it'll activate. However, if it isn't met, two things could happen. With LOT=false, the Taproot upgrade will expire, but a new activation period could be implemented if the community decides to try again with a new software version. With LOT=true, nodes will be-

---

[33]This transcript was written by Michael Folkson. The site contains many other transcripts from technical Bitcoin podcasts, conference talks, and even group conversations. Many of them are written by Bryan Bishop aka Kanzure, who is quite possibly one of the fastest typists on Earth. https://diyhpl.us/wiki/transcripts/bitcoin-magazine/2021-02-26-taproot-activation-lockinontimeout/

gin only accepting blocks that signal for the upgrade, which forces the activation.

Initially, in early 2021, there wasn't yet a Bitcoin Core release that would activate Taproot. Such a release was still pending community debate on what the appropriate activation mechanism should be. So this is a different context than during the UASF debate in 2017, where there *was* an existing Bitcoin Core BIP 9 deployment in the STARTED stage. Meanwhile, in early 2021, the discussion revolved around whether Bitcoin Core should switch from its usual BIP 9 deployment system to BIP 8, and if so, if LOT should be set to true or false.

The switch from BIP 9 to BIP 8 wasn't very controversial, as long as it stuck to the more conservative LOT=false incarnation. But it's not a no-brainer, because there's always a risk when making *any* change, especially to something as critical as the code that decides which rules apply to blocks. So it still raised the question: Is a switch to BIP 8 with LOT=false worth it?

It might be worth it to remain compatible with software from an independent group that insists on LOT=true (compatibility shouldn't be construed as endorsement). But this debate was never settled.[34]

The real controversy revolved around LOT=true.

A lot of people supported LOT=true because it made it so miners couldn't have a veto. The counterargument to that is that miners don't have a veto anyway; they can merely delay an orderly activation. This is because node owners can always switch to a new version of the node software that has a flag day, bypassing signaling altogether. But they'll

---

[34]There was pull request that implemented a transition from BIP 9 to BIP 8 in Bitcoin Core. This is a generic transition and not Taproot specific. However, it contained LOT=true code, which added complexity and triggered objections. A pure LOT=false version might have made it through review. https://github.com/bitcoin/bitcoin/pull/19573

have to wait.[35] If activation is delayed by a lack of signaling with `LOT=false`, the upgrade will expire after a year. After that, we could deploy any new upgrade mechanism, and potentially one without any signaling.

Another option could even be to start with `LOT=false`, wait half a year, and then say, "This is taking too long. Let's take a little more risk and set `LOT=true`."

The debate itself arguably ended up slowing down Taproot activation: There was no reason to believe miners would object to Taproot the way some did to SegWit, and there was no political drama around Taproot itself. It was very conceivable that a BIP 9 or BIP 8 with `LOT=false` activation would've gone smoothly, as it happened in the pre-SegWit era. But the debate created a stalemate, because Bitcoin Core generally doesn't ship functionality that's deemed controversial, and at that point, all activation options were controversial to at least some people.

It wasn't a stalemate because some people *preferred* `LOT=true`. Remember the RFC 7282 rough consensus process. As long as they didn't *object* to `LOT=false` (or BIP 9), then their preference for `LOT=true` could be dismissed. Because in that case, what would have remained were objections to `LOT=true` and no objections to `LOT=false`, and so you'd have moved forward with the thing nobody objected to.

But some people went beyond a mere preference for `LOT=true`. They claimed `LOT=false` was unsafe,[36] i.e. they objected to it. So we ended up with two proposals that both had objections. That these objections were advocated for by a very small number of developers was immaterial. They

---

[35]If the community doesn't wait until the timeout and activates a soft fork with a flag day, then anyone who doesn't upgrade to the new flag day software will think the soft fork failed to activate. Mandatory signaling avoids this need to wait, but at a cost.

[36]https://lists.linuxfoundation.org/pipermail/bitcoin-dev/2021-February/018498.html

needed to be addressed, e.g. shown to be incorrect or solved somehow. And that process could and did drag on for a while.

The Chain Split Scenario

The main objection to LOT=true was the same as the one raised against UASF: It could cause a chain split. Remember the reference above to MAD. An often-heard argument *for* LOT=true is that a chain split is so terrible — especially for miners who wouldn't be able to sell their new coins, it won't happen. They believe this is sufficient deterrence for miners to simply signal. Such game theory is beyond the scope of this book, but we can clarify what such a chain split would be like and why it's bad.

The following is one such example of how, if one part of the network runs LOT=true and another part runs LOT=false or an older version of the software, bad things could happen in the form of a chain split.

Let's say you're running the LOT=true version of Bitcoin Core and you want Taproot to activate. But the scenario here is that the rest of the world — including most miners — isn't doing this. The day arrives and you see a block that isn't signaling correctly but you want it to signal correctly, so you say "This block is now invalid, so I'm not going to accept this block. Instead, I'm just going to wait until another miner comes with a block that does meet my criteria." Maybe that happens once in every 10 blocks, so you're seeing new blocks, but they're coming in very, very slowly.

So far, you might think this is merely annoying. But now let's put some money on the line. What if you're trying to receive a payment?

Let's say somebody who runs a node with LOT=false sends you 1 BTC. So in this scenario, they're on a branch that's growing 10 times faster than the branch your node is seeing. Let's also say their blocks aren't completely full, so the sender uses a low fee rate. The transaction confirms quickly in their branch. But you're on this shorter, slower-moving branch, and all those transactions have to be squeezed into fewer blocks. Those blocks are completely full. In your branch, the transaction doesn't confirm. It's just sitting there in the mempool.

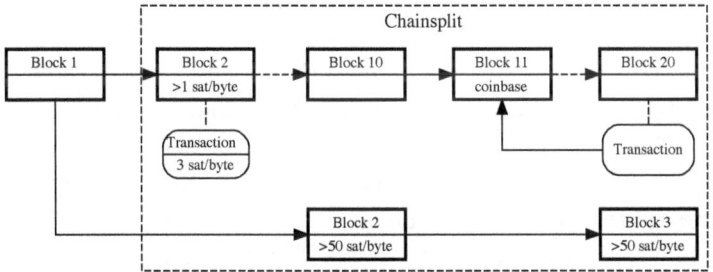

In this example, blocks on the fast moving side of the chain split require a fee of at least 1 satoshi per vbyte.[37] Due to congestion on the slower moving side, its minimum fee rate is 50 sat/vbyte. A transaction paying 3 sat/vbyte only confirms on one side of the split.

That's actually a relatively benevolent scenario. You've learned that you shouldn't accept unconfirmed transactions. You'll have a disagreement with your counterparty, you'll say, "It hasn't confirmed," and they'll say, "It has confirmed." Assuming you're aware of this chain split, you might realize what's going on.

If you had anticipated this situation, you would've asked your counterparty to pay a much higher fee than their node suggests (and maybe deduct it from the amount). Otherwise, you could've used something called Child Pays For Parent (CPFP) by taking their unconfirmed low fee transaction and spending it back to yourself with a very high fee transaction. The combined fee is then enough for miners to include both.

---

[37]https://bitcoin.stackexchange.com/a/89418/4948

A much worse scenario is when your counterparty is trying to send you coins that don't exist on your branch. How can that be? One possibility is that they're spending a coin that descends from a coin that was created by a miner on their branch. Every block contains a coinbase transaction, which sends the block subsidy (6.25 BTC at the time of writing), plus any transaction fees collected, to the miner. Each branch will have a different sequence of miners producing its blocks. This means each branch has unique coinbase transactions that don't exist on the other branch. That, in turn, means any transaction spending from such a coinbase transaction can't exist in the other branch.[38]

The general phenomenon described here is called transaction replay. In the case of a hard fork, it's often desirable to *prevent* transactions on one side of the fork from appearing (being replayed) on the other side. If this sounds fascinating, then you may like the author's presentation on the topic.[39] Otherwise, just understand that whether you want to prevent replay or guarantee it, it's a pain.

It's possible that the coins on both branches will have a different market price. In that case, the above examples become even more complicated, because you and your counterparty can't agree on what 1 BTC is worth.

In any case, translated to the RFC 7282 rough consensus process: If you propose something that creates the possibility of transaction replay, you should address how to deal with it.

But it gets worse.

Continuing with the above scenario of a short branch with LOT=true and a long branch with LOT=false, perhaps over time, the market price for coins on LOT=true increases.

---

[38]This can be used to generate something so called UTXO Fairy Dust. By deliberately spending a piece of that dust in a transaction, you can guarantee it won't replay on the other branch.

[39]https://sprovoost.nl/2017/11/10/a-short-history-of-replay-protection-2bd8b288cf94/

This price increase attracts miners, and this increase in mining activity increases the pace of block creation on this branch. In turn, it slows it down on the `LOT=false` branch.

This can lead to a tipping point if `LOT=true` overtakes the `LOT=false` branch. Your node chugs along just fine. It was following the `LOT=true` branch already when it was shorter, and it continues to do so now that it's longer.

But your friend in the other branch is about to have a very traumatic experience. Their node detects the longer branch. From its point of view, that branch is perfectly valid; the mandatory signaling on it doesn't violate any rules. So it's going to switch over!

This is very bad. Any transactions your friend had sent or received on their branch, if they don't also appear on your branch, will disappear. More accurately: Those transactions will either return to mempool, from which they could later end up getting confirmed again, or they could disappear entirely if they descend from a coinbase transaction.

Anything like a big reorganization[40] will cause mayhem, even without any malicious actors. Let's say a miner deposited coins on an exchange and your friend withdrew some coins from that same exchange. Exchanges generally don't allocate specific coins to specific users, so there's a chance the exchange used some of the miner coins to pay your friend. That means your friend never received that money and has to complain to the exchange. But if this happens on a large enough scale, the exchange is probably going to be insolvent.

Again translated to the RFC 7282 rough consensus process: Is it really enough to simply claim this scenario won't happen because of incentives to prevent it? Is it so unlikely that not even a contingency plan is needed to handle it? Some cities have nuclear shelters despite the MAD game theory, though others have indeed repurposed them as shop-

---

[40]https://en.bitcoin.it/wiki/Chain_Reorganization

ping malls. It seems like more of a political debate than a technical discussion.

Finally, it's worth pointing out that all the problems that `LOT=false` users are subjected to in world with `LOT=true` clients are also encountered by users who don't upgrade at all. Avoiding mandatory upgrades is also something to consider.

LOT=true Client, Rogue?

Ep. 36

This time around, the first software download release with the Taproot activation code wasn't Bitcoin Core. Instead, two developers decided to independently release a modified version of Bitcoin Core, which included BIP 8 and the `LOT=true` behavior.[41]

With open source software, anyone is free to release any variation of the software they want. Similarly, everyone is free to download whichever variation they want. However, in addition to the general objections to `LOT=true` above, there are other practical matters to think about when downloading such an alternative implementation. We cover these in the episode above. In particular, it's important to make sure you're not accidentally downloading malware (see chapter 9).

The Speedy Trial Proposal

To get out of this stalemate, Speedy Trial came to the rescue. It proposed[42] the following: "Rather than discussing whether or not there's going to be

---

[41]https://www.reddit.com/r/Bitcoin/comments/mruopv/bitcoinco released_bip8_lottrue_taproot_activation/

Ep. 31

[42]https://lists.linuxfoundation.org/pipermail/bitcoin-dev/2021-March/018583.html

signaling and having lots of arguments about it, let's just try it quickly." The proposed timeline[43] suggested the signaling would start in early May, last three months (until August), and then be activated three months later, in November.

Spoiler: As we mentioned at the beginning of the chapter, Taproot indeed activated on November 13, 2021.

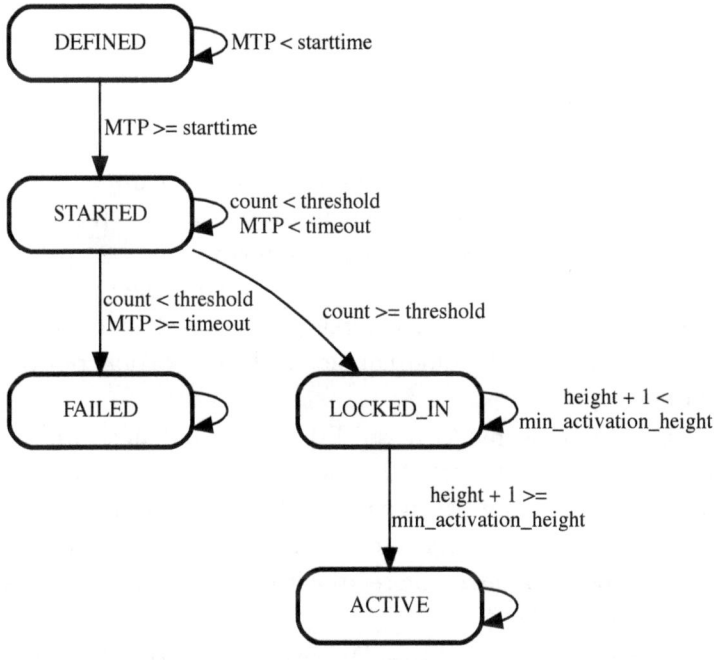

Speedy trial flow.

The diagram above is quite simple to understand. Compared to BIP 9 above, it only introduces one new concept: a minimum activation height. This adds a delay in the transition from LOCKED_IN to ACTIVE.

Although it's conceptually almost the same as BIP 9, the dates picked for Taproot are quite different than what

---

[43]https://lists.linuxfoundation.org/pipermail/bitcoin-dev/2021-March/018594.html

would've been picked before. The waiting period before signaling (DEFINED), as well as the signaling period (STARTED), are much shorter than usual (months instead of a full year). This way, we could know the result faster.

Knowing the result quickly is great, but the rush runs the risk of miners using fake signals rather than actually upgrading. So to add a margin of safety, the transition from LOCKED_IN to ACTIVE was increased from the usual single period (two weeks) to a fixed block height, which was expected to be reached in November 2021. That was the only code change required (a much smaller change than BIP 8).

So the "speedy" part refers to figuring out miner readiness, or at least to figuring out if there was any previously unknown miner objection, or just apathy. The rest of the process was slower, and it behaved a bit more like a flag day. Once the signal threshold was reached, the soft fork was set in stone, meaning it would happen, at least if people ran the full nodes.

This process made it so Taproot would activate six months after the initial release of the software, assuming 90 percent of miners were signaling. If that threshold wasn't met, the proposal would've expired, and activation options would've been discussed more, albeit with more data to back up decision making.

Speedy Trial seemed to sufficiently address the objections to BIP 9. From the objectors' point of view, because it was so fast, their own plans for BIP 8 wouldn't be delayed.

With the controversy (temporarily) out of the way, more developers came out of the woodwork and started writing code that could actually get Speedy Trial done.[44] In turn,

---

[44]Mainly https://github.com/bitcoin/bitcoin/pull/21377 ▦, https://github.com/bitcoin/bitcoin/pull/21686 ▦, and a BIP 8-based alternative that was briefly considered: https://github.com/bitcoin/bitcoin/pull/21392 ▦

because there were more developers from different angles cooperating on it and getting things done a little bit more quickly, it demonstrated that Speedy Trial was a good idea. When you have some disagreement, then people start procrastinating, not reviewing things, or not writing things. But if people begin working on something quickly and it's making progress, that's a vague indicator that it was a good choice.

We Have Taproot `LOCKED_IN`!

Ep. 40

Bitcoin Core v0.21.1 with the Speedy Trial code was released on May 1, 2021.[45]

The first retargeting period started a week before that release on April 24, 2021, and the threshold wasn't reached. The second retargeting period also didn't reach the threshold, but the third time was a charm. The 90 percent signaling threshold was reached on June 12, 2021, with `LOCKED_IN` happening a few days later.[46] It lasted until the November activation.

Remember that the signal for a soft fork (BIP 9, BIP 8, or Speedy Trial) is just a bit flag in the block header. Miners can and do use custom software to set this bit. At the same time, miners run full nodes that actually enforce the consensus rules. But if they don't upgrade their own nodes, then their outdated nodes will simply ignore the flag, and their nodes won't enforce the new rules. For that to happen, they need to actually upgrade their node software.

In general, it's preferred if miners actually upgrade their nodes and don't fake signal. That's one reason why the timeout in BIP 9 was so long. But because Speedy Trial happened on such short notice, some may have considered it

---

[45]https://bitcoincore.org/en/2021/05/01/release-0.21.1/
[46]https://sports.yahoo.com/locked-bitcoin-taproot-upgrade-gets-120837972.html

too risky to upgrade their software. Others ran into practical issues performing the upgrade. Mining pool operator Alejandro De La Torre described some of the practical issues he encountered in the field on a podcast episode.[47]

The accompanying episode goes into further detail about what, once Taproot activation became inevitable, needed to happen before it could ultimately be used on the Bitcoin network safely. We also explain how upcoming Bitcoin Core releases will handle the Taproot upgrade, especially with respect to its wallet software. At the time of writing, there's some basic Taproot wallet support, but it's still a work in progress.

Moving Forward

Because Speedy Trial was successful, it's possible we can use it as a template for soft fork activation moving forward. Or, we could interpret the lack of drama as an argument to just stick with BIP 9 or a `LOT=false` version of BIP 8. Perhaps some aspects of `LOT=true` deployment can be made safer.

Even if it's inherently unsafe, it could make sense to continue developing it further, having the code already in place in case it's ever needed. Perhaps the Bitcoin Core software could have generic support for it, even if the project itself recommends against using it. The best time to think about such matters is when they're not yet needed.

Burying Soft Forks

After all is said and done and a soft fork has activated, what do you do with the activation code? Is it merely a scaffold that can be removed

---

[47]https://stephanlivera.com/episode/277/
Ep. 54

once the new rules are active? Or is the activation mechanism itself a permanent part of the rules?

As was done with previous soft forks, it looks like a future Bitcoin Core release will "bury" the Taproot activation. This means the node will treat the Taproot rules as if they've been active since Bitcoin's very beginning. This is possible because, when applying these rules retroactively, only one historical block does not conform to them. This block can be grandfathered in.[48]

In the episode we explain what the benefits are of burying a soft fork, in particular pointing out how it helps developers when they review the Bitcoin Core codebase or when they perform tests on it.

After that, we outline a potential edge case scenario where burying soft forks could, in a worst-case scenario, split the Bitcoin blockchain between upgraded and non-upgraded nodes. Bitcoin Core developers generally don't consider this edge case — a very long block re-org — to be a realistic problem and/or believe that this would be such a big problem that a buried soft fork would be a minor concern comparatively. However, as we explain, not everyone agrees with this assessment entirely.

---

[48]https://github.com/bitcoin/bitcoin/pull/23536

Appendix

Appendix A

More Episodes

Not all episodes of *Bitcoin, Explained* made it into this book. Here are some other episodes you could listen to. The descriptions below are mostly based on the show notes written by co-host Aaron van Wirdum.

Basics

What Is an xpub?

Ep. 07

In this episode, we explain what an extended public key (xpub) is and how it's used by Bitcoin wallets. Extended keys were first introduced in BIP 32 to create so-called hierarchical deterministic wallets.[1] Such wallets create a fresh address each time the user wants to receive coins. Unlike earlier wallets that required a fresh backup for every address, these new wallets only require a single backup, usually in the form of the familiar 12-24 word mnemonic.[2]

---

[1] https://en.bitcoin.it/wiki/BIP_0032

[2] BIP 39 https://en.bitcoin.it/wiki/BIP_0039

Replace-By-Fee (RBF)

Ep. 26

In this episode, we explain Replace-By-Fee (RBF). RBF is a trick that lets unconfirmed transactions be replaced with conflicting transactions that include a higher fee.

With RBF, users can essentially bump a transaction fee to incentivize miners to include a transaction in a block. We detail three advantages of RBF: the option to "speed up" a transaction (1), which can in turn result in a more effective fee market for block space (2), and the potential to make more efficient use of block space by updating transactions to include more recipients (3).

The main disadvantage of RBF is that it makes it slightly easier to double-spend unconfirmed transactions, which was also at the root of a "double-spend" controversy that dominated headlines in early 2021.[3] We discuss some solutions to diminish this risk, including "opt-in RBF," which is currently implemented in Bitcoin Core.

Finally, we explain in some detail how opt-in RBF works and which conditions must be met before a transaction is considered replaceable. In the process, we note some complications with this version of RBF — for example, in the context of the Lightning network.

---

[3]https://insights.deribit.com/market-research/was-there-a-bitcoin-double-spend-on-jan-20-2021/

Signet

Ep. 10

A signet is a new type of testnet for Bitcoin. In this episode, we discuss the original version of the public testing blockchain (testnet) and outline its problems. We then explain how signets are similar in nature to testnet, but more reliable and centrally controlled. A signet — there can be more than one — achieves this by adding an additional signature requirement to block validation (hence "sig").[4]

Mempools, Child Pays For Parent, and Package Relay

Ep. 19

In this episode, we discuss Bitcoin memory pools (mempools), Child Pays For Parent (CPFP), and package relay.

Package relay is the project Gloria Zhao is working on as part of her Brink fellowship.[5]. It would make the Lightning network more robust (among other benefits). Mempools are the collections of unconfirmed transactions stored by nodes. Nodes then forward these unconfirmed transactions from their mempool to peers. Miners usually select the transactions from their mempool that include the highest fees to include these in the blocks they mine.

However, mempools can get full, at which point transactions that pay the lowest fees are ejected. This is actually a problem in the context of CPFP, which is a trick that lets users speed up low-fee transactions by spending the coins from those transactions in a new transaction with a high fee to compensate.[6] Tricks like these can be particularly

---

[4]Read more about signet(s), or try it for yourself: https://en.bitco in.it/wiki/Signet

[5]https://brink.dev/programs

[6]https://bitcoinops.org/en/topics/cpfp/

important in the context of time-sensitive protocols like the Lightning network.

In this episode, we go into detail about how package relay could enable CPFP — even in cases where low-fee transactions are dropped from mempools — by bundling transactions into packets. We also explore why this may be easier said than done.

Death to the Mempool, Long Live the Mempool

Ep. 50

We discuss a recent thread on the Bitcoin development mailing list, titled "Death to the Mempool, Long Live the Mempool."[7]

In the thread, Blockstream engineer Lisa "niftynei" Neigut proposes getting rid of the memory pool (mempool), which is the collection of unconfirmed transactions that Bitcoin nodes use to share transactions over the network and that Bitcoin miners use to create new blocks from. She argues that the Bitcoin system could be drastically simplified if users instead just send their transactions directly to miners (or mining pools).

In the episode, we explain how this would work and why this isn't as simple as it may sound. We address the responses in the thread, going over the reasons why getting rid of the mempool is in fact not a very good solution for a system like Bitcoin. There's a specific focus on the implications this would have on mining privacy and decentralization. It also explores some other tradeoffs that would need to be made to make the Bitcoin system work without a mempool.

---

[7]https://lists.linuxfoundation.org/pipermail/bitcoin-dev/2021-October/019572.html

Bitcoin Improvement Proposal (BIP) Process

Ep. 39

In this episode, we explain what Bitcoin Improvement Proposals (BIPs) are and how the BIP process works. We discuss why the BIP process is a useful yet non-binding convention within Bitcoin's technical community.

First, we explain what a BIP is exactly— and what it isn't. We also explain that only improvements to Bitcoin software that affect other projects require a BIP. We then dive into the history of the BIP process a little bit, noting that the format was introduced by Libbitcoin developer Amir Taaki, and later updated by Bitcoin Knots maintainer Luke Dashjr.

Finally, we explain how the BIP process itself works — that is, how a proposal can be turned into a BIP and eventually be implemented in software. We also briefly explain how the BIP process could become corrupted and why that wouldn't be a very big deal.

Resource Usage

Compact Client-Side Filtering (Neutrino)

Ep. 25

In this episode, we discuss Compact Client-Side Filtering, also known as Neutrino. This is a solution to use Bitcoin without needing to download and validate the entire blockchain and without sacrificing your privacy to someone who operates a full node (and therefore did download and validate the entire blockchain).

Downloading and validating the entire Bitcoin blockchain can take a couple of days even on a standard laptop, and it takes much longer on smartphones and other limited-performance computers. This is why many people prefer to use light clients. These aren't quite as secure as full Bitcoin nodes, but they do require fewer computational resources to operate.

Some types of light clients — Simplified Payment Verification (SPV) clients — essentially ask nodes on the Bitcoin network about the particular Bitcoin addresses they're interested in to check how much bitcoin they own. This is bad for privacy, since the full node operator learns which addresses belong to the SPV user.

Compact Client-Side Filtering is a newer solution to accomplish goals similar to SPV, but without the loss of privacy. This works, in short, by having full node operators create a cryptographic data structure that tells the light client user whether a block could've contained activity pertaining to its addresses, so the user can keep track of its funds by downloading only a small subset of all Bitcoin blocks.

We explain how this works in more detail, and we discuss some of the tradeoffs of this solution.

Compact Blocks

We explain how Bitcoin's peer-to-peer network is made more efficient and faster with compact blocks.[8]

Compact blocks are — as the name suggests — compact versions of Bitcoin blocks that have been used by Bitcoin Core nodes since version 0.13. Compact blocks contain the minimal amount of data required for Bitcoin nodes to reconstruct entire blocks. Most notably, compact blocks exclude most transaction data to instead include short transaction identifiers. Bitcoin nodes can use these short identifiers to figure out which transactions from their mempools should be included in the blocks.

Ep. 51

We explain how and why compact blocks benefit the Bitcoin network, and specifically how they help counter mining centralization. We also cover some edge cases that can result from the use of compact blocks — like the possibility that different valid transactions can have an identical identifier — and how Bitcoin nodes handle such occurrences.

You may also want to watch Greg Maxwell's presentation about advances in block propagation, or read the transcript.[9]

---

[8]https://bitcoincore.org/en/2016/06/07/compact-blocks-faq/
[9]https://btctranscripts.com/greg-maxwell/gmaxwell-2017-11-27-advances-in-block-propagation/

Erlay

Ep. 34

In this episode, we discuss the Erlay protocol. Erlay is a proposal to reduce the bandwidth required to run a Bitcoin node. It was proposed and developed by University of British Columbia researchers Gleb Naumenko, Alexandra Fedorova, and Ivan Beschastnikh; Blockstream engineer Pieter Wuille; and independent Bitcoin Core contributor Gregory Maxwell.

Bitcoin nodes use bandwidth to receive and transmit both block data and transaction data. Reducing the amount of bandwidth a node requires to do this would make it cheaper to run a node. Alternatively, it would allow nodes to connect to more peers without increasing bandwidth usage.

We explain that Erlay uses set reconciliation to reduce the amount of data nodes need to share transactions. More specifically, Erlay uses a mathematical trick called Minisketch[10]. This solution is based on preexisting mathematical formulas used in biometrics technology.

We also outline how this trick is applied in the context of Bitcoin to let different nodes sync their mempools, which are the sets of transactions they've received in anticipation of a new block — or, in the case of a miner, to include in a new block.

---

[10]https://github.com/sipa/minisketch

Attacks

Time-Warp Attack

In this episode, we explain the "time-warp attack" on Bitcoin. A potential fix for this attack is included in Matt Corallo's proposed Great Consensus Cleanup soft fork,[11] which — at the time of writing — hasn't seen much progress.

Ep. 05

PSBT and RBF Attacks

In this episode, we break down and explain Partially Signed Bitcoin Transactions (PSBT) and Replace-By-Fee (RBF), along with some really tricky attacks that were discovered.[12]

Ep. 01   PSBT is a data format that allows wallets and other tools to exchange information about a Bitcoin transaction and the signatures necessary to complete it.[13]

---

[11] https://github.com/TheBlueMatt/bips/blob/cleanup-softfork/bip-XXXX.mediawiki

[12] PSBT Attack Vector https://blog.trezor.io/latest-firmware-updates-correct-possible-segwit-transaction-vulnerability-266df0d2860 and RBF Attack Vector https://zengo.com/bigspender-double-spend-vulnerability-in-bitcoin-wallets/

[13] https://bitcoinops.org/en/topics/psbt/

Mining Pool Censorship

Ep. 37

In this episode, we discuss the emergence of Mara Pool, the American Bitcoin mining pool, which — at the time we recorded this episode — claimed to be fully compliant with US regulations. This means it applies anti-money laundering (AML) checks and adheres to the sanction list of the Office of Foreign Assets Control (OFAC). While details haven't been made explicit, this presumably means that this pool won't include transactions in blocks if these transactions send coin to or from Bitcoin addresses that have been included on an OFAC blacklist.

Some time after recording, it changed course and announced it wouldn't be censoring transactions.

In the episode, we discuss the prospects of mining censorship, what that would mean for Bitcoin, and what can be done about it. We expand upon what it could look like if this practice is adopted more widely. We consider what censoring mining pools could accomplish if they ever get close to controlling a majority of hash power and what Bitcoin users could potentially do in such a scenario (if anything).

Wallets

Hardware Wallet Integration in Bitcoin Core

Ep. 30

We discuss hardware wallet integration into Bitcoin Core, which is one of the ongoing projects that Sjors regularly contributes to.

Hardware wallets are a popular solution for storing private keys offline to minimize the risk that hackers gain access to the corresponding coins. They're used in combination with regular software wallets to sign transactions in such a way that the private keys never leave the device.

Hardware Wallet Security and Jade

Ep. 43

Co-host Aaron is joined by Blockstream's Lawrence Nahum, one of the developers of the Jade hardware wallet, and Ben Kaufman, one of the developers of Spectre Desktop — a software tool for hardware wallets.

They talk about what hardware wallets are and discuss the design tradeoffs that different hardware wallets have taken by focusing on the Trezor, Ledger, and Coldcard devices specifically. In this light, Lawrence and Ben explain what secure elements and secure chips are and why some hardware wallets choose to rely on using such chips more than others.

Then, Lawrence explains which tradeoffs Jade Wallet makes. He also details how an additional server-based security step is used to further secure Jade Wallet, and he briefly outlines some additional differences in hardware wallet designs— for example, those focused on usability.

Finally, they discuss whether hardware wallets are overrated, or if you might as well use a dedicated smartphone to store your bitcoin.

Bitcoin Beach

Ep. 42

Co-host Aaron speaks with Bitcoin Beach Wallet developer Nicolas Burtey in El Zonte, El Salvador — which has been dubbed Bitcoin Beach — to discuss the Bitcoin Beach Wallet, a Bitcoin and Lightning wallet specifically designed for use in the small Central American coastal town frequented by surfers and, now, bitcoiners.

They discuss the pros and cons of custodial and non-custodial Lightning wallets, and Nicolas explains why he opted to make the Bitcoin Beach Wallet a shared-custodial wallet, and what that means exactly.

They go on to discuss some of the design decisions and tradeoffs that the Bitcoin Beach Wallet has made, which include ledger-based payments between Bitcoin Beach Wallet users, and webpage-based zero invoice payments to facilitate payments from other Lightning wallets. Nicolas also speculates about a potential cross-wallet user account system to further improve the Lightning user experience over time.

Finally, there's discussion of some of the subtle incompatibilities between different Lightning wallets that use different techniques for routing payments, privacy considerations versus user experience in a community like El Zonte's, and more.

Chivo

Ep. 46

In this episode, we discuss the Chivo application, the Bitcoin wallet, and the payment terminal provided by the government of El Salvador. The Chivo app is closed source software. Instead of analyzing the source code and design of the application, we had to rely on personal experience with the wallet and payment terminal.

The episode opens with some general information about

the Chivo Wallet, like why it was developed and who developed it (insofar anything is known about that). We discuss Aaron's experiences with the wallet and speculate what that means for the design. After that, we discuss the design of the payment terminal that's included in the application, and we also briefly touch on the Chivo ATMs that have been deployed across the country. Finally, we discuss the difference in philosophy between the design of the Chivo application and Bitcoin's free and open source software culture.

Payment Pools

Ep. 06

In this episode, we explain what payment pools are and why they need Taproot. We discuss the user experience of sharing UTXOs and how payment pools can work with the Lightning network. For more information, see Aaron's article.[14]

Accounts with Easypaysy

Ep. 11

We discuss Jose Femenias' easypaysy proposal, an account system for Bitcoin, on Bitcoin. One feature it supports is stealth address identities. We discuss several use cases. Finally, we explain what non-repudiation is.

Aaron also wrote an article covering easypaysy for Bitcoin Magazine.[15]

---

[14]https://bitcoinmagazine.com/articles/building-on-taproot-payment-pools-could-be-bitcoins-next-layer-two-protocol

[15]https://bitcoinmagazine.com/articles/bitcoin-need-accounts-one-developer-thinks-figured

Lightning

One could write an entire book about the Lightning network. And in fact, others have, see e.g. *Mastering the Lightning Network: A Second Layer Blockchain Protocol for Instant Bitcoin Payments* by Andreas M. Antonopoulos and Olaoluwa Osuntokun (aka Roasbeef).[16]

This book doesn't cover Lightning, but several *Bitcoin, Explained* episodes did.

Basics

Ep. 22

We discuss the basics of the Lightning network, Bitcoin's Layer 2 protocol for cheaper, faster, and potentially more private transactions. We explain that the Lightning network works as a scaling layer because it lets users make off-chain transactions through bidirectional payment channels: Two users can pay one another an arbitrary number of times without these transactions being recorded on the blockchain. We went on to explain how, in the Lightning protocol, these off-chain transactions are secure — that is, how each of the participants is at any point guaranteed to claim their respective funds from the payment channel.

Then we explain how bidirectional payment channels can be linked across a network of users to extend the potential of off-chain transactions so any Lightning user can pay any other Lightning user, even if they haven't set up a payment channel between the two of them specifically.

Finally, we briefly touch on some of the challenges presented by the Lightning network — most notably the requirement of payment channels to have sufficient liquidity locked into them.

---

[16]https://www.oreilly.com/library/view/mastering-the-lightning/9781492054856/

RBF Bug in Bitcoin Core

Ep. 38

We discuss CVE-2021-31876, a bug in the Bitcoin Core code that affects Replace-By-Fee (RBF) child transactions.[17] The Common Vulnerabilities and Exposures (CVE) system offers an overview of publicly known software bugs. A new bug in the Bitcoin Core code was discovered and disclosed by Antoine Riard, and it was added to the CVE overview.

We explain that the bug affects how RBF logic is handled by the Bitcoin Core software. When one unconfirmed transaction includes an RBF flag (which means it should be considered replaceable if a conflicting transaction with a higher fee is broadcast over the network), any following transaction that spends coins from the original transaction should also be considered replaceable — even if the second transaction doesn't itself have an RBF flag. Bitcoin Core software wouldn't do this, however, which means the second transaction would in fact not be considered replaceable.

This is a fairly innocent bug; in most cases, the second transaction will still confirm eventually, while there are also other solutions to speed confirmation up if the included fee is too low. But in very specific cases, like some fallback security mechanisms on the Lightning network, the bug could in fact cause complications. We try to explain what such a scenario would look like, but we end up totally confused.

---

[17]https://cve.mitre.org/cgi-bin/cvename.cgi?name=CVE-2021-31876

Routing

Ep. 41

We're joined by Lightning developer Joost Jager to discuss everything about Lightning network routing.

The Lightning network consists of a network of payment channels. Each payment channel exists between two Lightning users. But even if two users don't have a payment channel between themselves directly, they can pay each other through one or several other Lightning users, who in that case forward the payment from the payer to the payee.

The challenge is that they need to find a payment path across the network that allows the funds to move from the payer to the payee — ideally the cheapest, fastest, and most reliable payment path available.

Joost explains how Lightning nodes currently construct a map of the Lightning network and what information about all of the (publicly visible) payment channels is included in that map. Next, he outlines on what basis Lightning nodes calculate the best path over the network to reach the payee and how the performance of this route factors into future path-finding calculations.

Finally, we discuss some (potential) optimizations to benefit Lightning network routing, such as rebalancing schemes and trampoline payments.

Optimally Reliable and Cheap Payment Flows on the Lightning Network

Ep. 47

In this episode, we interview another expert on Lightning routing, René Pickhardt. We discuss his paper *Optimally Reliable & Cheap Payment Flows on the Lightning Network.*[18] To cite the abstract:

Today, payment paths in Bitcoin's Lightning Network are found by searching for shortest paths on the fee graph. We enhance this approach in two dimensions. Firstly, we take into account the probability of a payment actually being possible due to the unknown balance distributions in the channels. Secondly, we use minimum cost flows as a proper generalization of shortest paths to multi-part payments (MPP). In particular we show that under plausible assumptions about the balance distributions we can find the most likely MPP for any given set of senders, recipients and amounts by solving for a (generalized) integer minimum cost flow with a separable and convex cost function. Polynomial time exact algorithms as well as approximations are known for this optimization problem. We present a round-based algorithm of min-cost flow computations for delivering large payment amounts over the Lightning Network. This algorithm works by updating the probability distributions with the information gained from both successful and unsuccessful paths on prior rounds. In all our experiments a single digit number of rounds sufficed

---

[18]https://arxiv.org/abs/2107.05322

to deliver payments of sizes that were close to the total local balance of the sender. Early experiments indicate that our approach increases the size of payments that can be reliably delivered by several orders of magnitude compared to the current state of the art. We observe that finding the cheapest multi-part payments is an NP-hard problem considering the current fee structure and propose dropping the base fee to make it a linear min-cost flow problem. Finally, we discuss possibilities for maximizing the probability while at the same time minimizing the fees of a flow. While this turns out to be a hard problem in general as well - even in the single path case - it appears to be surprisingly tractable in practice.

Eltoo and SIGHASH_ANYPREVOUT

We covered this topic twice, so there are two episodes to choose from. In episode 35, we explain what this is, and in episode 48, one of the authors, c-lightning developer Christian Decker, joins us to explain it in his words.

Ep. 35

First, we discuss SIGHASH_ANYPREVOUT, a proposed new sighash flag that would enable a cleaner version of the Lightning network and other Layer 2 protocols. Sighash flags are included in Bitcoin transactions to indicate which part of the transaction is signed by the required private keys.

This can be (almost) the entire transaction or specific parts of it. Signing only specific parts allows for some flexibility to adjust the transaction even after it's signed, which can sometimes be useful. We explain that SIGHASH_ANYPREVOUT is a new type of sighash flag that would sign most of the transaction, but not the inputs. This means that the inputs could be swapped, as long as the new inputs would still be compatible with the signature.

SIGHASH_ANYPREVOUT would be especially useful in context of Eltoo, a proposed Layer 2 protocol that would enable a new version of the Lightning network. Where Lightning users currently need to store old channel data for security reasons and could also be punished severely if they accidentally broadcast some of this data at the wrong time, we discuss how SIGHASH_ANYPREVOUT would do away with this requirement.

Ep. 48

Bolt 12 — Recurring Payments, Etc.

We discuss Basis of Lightning Technology 12 (BOLT 12), a newly proposed Lightning network specification for "offers," which are a type of "meta invoices" designed by c-lightning developer Rusty Russell.

Ep. 44

Where coins on Bitcoin's base layer are sent to addresses, the Lightning network uses invoices. Invoices communicate the requested amount, the node destination, and the hash of a secret that's used for payment routing. This works, but it has a number of limitations — notably that the amount must be bitcoin-denominated (as opposed to fiat denominated), and the invoice can only be used once.

BOLT 12, which has been implemented in c-lightning, is a way to essentially refer a payer to the node that is to be paid, in order to request a new invoice. While the BOLT 12 offer can be static and reusable — it always refers to the same node — the payee can generate new invoices on the fly when requested, allowing for much more flexibility.

Finally, we discuss how the new BOLT 12 messages are communicated over the Lightning network through an update to the BOLT 7 specification for message relay.

Sidechains and More

Lightning isn't the only path forward for scaling Bitcoin, though it's the most actively developed one at the moment. Sidechains are another approach, and they can optionally be combined with Lightning.

Though there's no universally agreed upon definition of what a sidechain is, the general idea is that you create a separate blockchain with its own rules that's somehow pegged to the Bitcoin blockchain. The advantage of this approach, in theory, is that only nodes that care about a particular sidechain need to verify it, while the rest of the network only needs to check that the amount of bitcoin leaving the sidechain doesn't exceed the amount going in.

We discussed several of these ideas in the podcast, often with the help of Utrecht-based ad hoc co-host Ruben Somsen.

Drivechains

Drivechain is a sidechain project spearheaded by Paul Sztorc.[19]

This should make the sidechain coins interchangeable with bitcoin and therefore, they should carry an equal value. In a way, sidechains let users "move" bitcoin across blockchains, where they're subject to different protocol rules, allowing for greater transaction capacity, more privacy, and other benefits. We explain that Drivechain consists of two main innovations.

Ep. 23

The first is Blind Merged Mining (BMM), which lets Bitcoin miners secure the drivechain with their existing hash power, but without necessarily needing to validate everything that happens on the sidechain.

The second is Hashrate Escrows, which lets miners "move" coins from the Bitcoin blockchain to the sidechain and back.

---

[19]https://www.drivechain.info

We also discuss some of the benefits and complications with Drivechain — most notably the security implications of letting miners control the pegging out process. We consider the arguments of why this process is incentive compatible (which is important for security) — or why it might not be.

Perpetual One-Way Peg

Ep. 12

Ruben explains his proposal to combine Blind Merged Mining and Perpetual One-Way Pegs to create a new type of sidechain. The bad news: It won't make you rich, but it could help scale Bitcoin!

First, he introduces the concept of a blind merge-mind chain. He then explains the use cases for the perpetual one-way peg and what Merge Mining is. We then get to Perpetual One-Way Peg and try answer the question: Why would the sidechain coin be worth anything?

A blog post by Ruben also explains the concept.[20]

Softchains

Ep. 27

This time, we discuss one of Ruben's own proposals: Softchains.[21]

Softchains are a type of two-way peg sidechains that utilize a new type of consensus mechanism: proof-of-work fraud proofs (or as Sjors prefers to call them, proof-of-work fraud indicators). Using this consensus mechanism, users don't validate the content of each block, but instead only check the proof-of-work header, like Simplified Payment Verification (SPV) clients do. But using proof-of-work fraud

---

[20]https://medium.com/@RubenSomsen/21-million-bitcoins-to-rule-all-sidechains-the-perpetual-one-way-peg-96cb2f8ac302

[21]https://lists.linuxfoundation.org/pipermail/bitcoin-dev/2020-December/018331.html

proofs, users do validate the entire content of blocks any time a blockchain fork occurs. This offers a security model in between full node security and SPV security.

Ruben explains that by using proof-of-work fraud proofs for sidechains to create Softchains, Bitcoin full nodes could validate entire sidechains at minimal cost. This new model might be useful for certain types of sidechains, most notably "block size increase" sidechains that do nothing fancy but do offer more transaction capacity. We also discuss some of the downsides of the Softchain model.

Statechains

We discuss yet another one of Ruben's proposals: Statechains on Bitcoin. Statechains allow you to send keys instead of UTXOs, and they offer quite a few scaling and functionality improvements.

Ep. 08

You might also want to refer to Ruben's presentation[22] in Bitcoin Magazine about Statechains, as well as Aaron's Bitcoin Magazine article.[23]

RSK, Federated Sidechains, and Powpeg

We discuss RSK's shift from a federated sidechain model to the project's new Powpeg solution.

RSK is a merge-mined, Ethereum-like Bitcoin sidechain developed by IOVLabs. Bitcoin users can effectively move their coins to this blockchain

Ep. 20

that operates more like Ethereum and move the coins back to the Bitcoin blockchain when they so choose. Some Bitcoin miners utilize their hash power to mine blocks

---

[22]https://youtu.be/CKx6eULIC3A

[23]https://bitcoinmagazine.com/articles/statechains-sending-keys-not-coins-to-scale-bitcoin-off-chain

on the sidechain and earn some extra transaction fees by doing so.

The tricky part of any sidechain is allowing users to securely move their coins between blockchains. This is technically done by locking coins on the Bitcoin blockchain and issuing corresponding coins on the sidechain, and vice versa: locking coins on the sidechain to unlock the coins on the Bitcoin blockchain.

So far, RSK has done this by locking the coins into a multi-signature address, for which the private keys were controlled by a group of well-known companies (known as a federated sidechain model). A majority was needed to unlock the coins, which they were to only do if and when the corresponding sidechain coins were locked.

RSK is now switching to a Powpeg model where the keys to the multi-signature address are controlled by special tamper-proof hardware modules that are in turn programmed to only unlock coins on the Bitcoin blockchain if and when the corresponding coins on the sidechain are locked, and the transactions to lock these coins up have a significant number of confirmations.

We explain how this works exactly, and we discuss some of Powpeg's security tradeoffs.

More Stuff on the Chain

RGB

Ep. 33

We're joined by Ruben Somsen to discuss RGB tokens, a Layer 2 protocol for Bitcoin to support alternative currency and token schemes (like the currently popular non-fungible tokens, or NFTs). We explain that the Bitcoin blockchain has been (ab)used by users to host data since the project's early days. This was initially done through otherwise-useless transaction outputs, which meant that all Bitcoin users had to store this data locally. A feature called OP_RETURN later limited this burden. We also explain that people have been using the Bitcoin blockchain to host alternative currency and token schemes for a long time.

A few years ago, Sjors also gave a presentation about RGB and earlier attempts at using the Bitcoin blockchain to store non-money things.[24]

OpenTimestamps

Ep. 16

In this episode, we discuss OpenTimestamps,[25] a Bitcoin-based time stamping project by applied cryptography consultant and former Bitcoin Core contributor Peter Todd. OpenTimestamps leverages the security of the Bitcoin blockchain to timestamp any type of data, allowing for irrefutable proof that that data existed at a particular point in time.

We explain that virtually any amount of data can, in fact, be timestamped in the Bitcoin blockchain at minimal cost because OpenTimestamps leverages Merkle trees, the cryptographic trick to aggregate data into a single, compact

---

[24]https://www.youtube.com/watch?v=PgeqT6ruBWU
[25]https://opentimestamps.org

hash. This hash is then included in a Bitcoin transaction, making all of the data aggregated into the hash as immutable as any other Bitcoin transaction.

Around the time the episode was recorded, Peter offered an interesting showcase of OpenTimestamps, as he proved that the public key used by Google to sign a controversial email to Hunter Biden existed as early as 2016.[26]

We also discuss some of the other possibilities that a time-stamping system like OpenTimestamps offers, as well as its limitations. Finally, Aaron provides a little bit of context for the history of cryptographic time stamping, which was itself referenced in the Bitcoin white paper.

We timestamped the source code for this book, so you can verify that a draft version existed as early as March 2022:

```
c=86a7cd200acb1812b6b2f8be27c8380ea44c9470
git verify-commit $c
git cat-file -p $c > meta/commit
ots verify meta/commit.ots
```

The above verification script is also in the source code repository, along with the `.ots` timestamp file that you need to verify it: https://btcwip.com/ots ▦

Discreet Log Contracts

Ep. 53

In this episode, we're again joined by resident sidechain and Layer 2 expert Ruben Somsen, this time to discuss Discreet Log Contracts (DLCs).

Discreet Log Contracts are a type of smart contracts for Bitcoin, first proposed by Lightning network white paper coauthor Tadge Dryja.[27] In

---

[26] https://github.com/robertdavidgraham/hunter-dkim/tree/main/ots-timestamp ▦

[27] https://adiabat.github.io/dlc.pdf ▦

essence, DLCs are a way to perform bets — but this means they can ultimately be leveraged for all sorts of financial instruments, including futures markets, insurances, and stablecoins.

At the start of the episode, we discuss what can be considered a type of proto-DLC — namely a multi-signature setup for sports betting where two participants add a neutral third party (an "oracle") that can resolve the bet one way or the other if needed. However, we explain how this solution comes with a number of downsides, like the difficulty of scaling it.

From there, we go on to explain how DLCs solved these problems using a setup that resembles payment channels as used on the Lightning network. When structured like this, oracles merely need to publish a cryptographically signed message about the outcome of an event, which can be used by the winning participant of the bet to create a withdrawal transaction from the payment channel.

Finally, we explain how the original DLC concept could be streamlined by using adaptor signatures,[28] a sort of "incomplete signature" that can be made complete using the signed message from the oracle. With adaptor signatures, DLCs no longer require a separate withdrawal transaction, as the winner can claim funds from the payment channel directly.

---

[28]https://bitcoinops.org/en/topics/adaptor-signatures/

Software Releases

Bitcoin Core v0.21

Ep. 24

In this episode, we discuss Bitcoin Core 0.21.0, the 21st major release of the Bitcoin Core software.[29] Bitcoin Core is the oldest and most important Bitcoin node implementation, which is often also regarded as the reference implementation for the Bitcoin protocol.

Guided by the Bitcoin Core 0.21.0 release notes, we discuss this release's most important changes. These include the new mempool policy for rebroadcasting transactions, Tor v3 support, peer anchors for when the node restarts, BIP 157 (Neutrino) for light clients, the new testnet called Signet, BIP 339 (wtxid relay), Taproot code, RPC changes including a new send RPC, ZeroMQ, descriptor wallets, the new SQLite database system, and the satoshi-per-byte fee denomination.

For each of the new features, we discuss what the features are, how they'll change using Bitcoin (Core), and — where applicable — what the end goal is. (In Bitcoin Core development, new features are often part of a bigger process.) For any feature we discussed on a previous episode of *Bitcoin, Explained*, we also mention the relevant episode number.

---

[29]https://bitcoinmagazine.com/technical/bitcoin-core-0-21-0-released-whats-new

Bitcoin Core v22.0

Ep. 45

In this episode, we discuss Bitcoin Core 22.0, the next major release of the Bitcoin Core software client.[30]

The first of these is hardware wallet support in the graphical user interface (GUI). While hardware wallet support has been rolling out across several previous Bitcoin Core releases, it's now fully available in the GUI. The second highlighted upgrade is support for the Invisible Internet Project (I2P), a Tor-like internet privacy layer. We also briefly touch on the differences between I2P and Tor.

The third upgrade discussed in the episode is Taproot support. While Taproot activation logic was already included in Bitcoin Core 0.21.1, Bitcoin Core 22.0 is the first major Bitcoin Core release ready to support Taproot, albeit with limited functionality.

The fourth upgrade we discuss is an update to the `testmempoolaccept` logic, which paves the way toward a bigger package relay upgrade. This could, in a future release, allow transactions to be transmitted over the Bitcoin network in packages including several transactions at the same time.

Additionally, we briefly discuss an extension to multisig address creation, the new NAT-PMP option, and more.

---

[30]https://bitcoincore.org/en/releases/22.0/

Syncing Old Bitcoin Nodes

Ep. 55

We discuss research done by CasaHODL cofounder and CTO Jameson Lopp, as well as research done by Sjors on syncing old Bitcoin nodes.[31]

Whenever a new Bitcoin node comes online, it must first sync with the rest of the Bitcoin network: It needs to download and verify the entire blockchain up until the most recent block to be up to date on the state of bitcoin ownership. This can take quite a while, however, and it should take longer over time as the blockchain keeps growing. To offset this, and to improve user experience more generally, Bitcoin Core developers seek to improve performance of the Bitcoin Core code so that newer releases sync faster than their predecessors.

In the episode, we outline the performance improvements of Bitcoin Core clients over time, as analyzed most recently in two blog posts by Jameson. We first explain why some very old Bitcoin clients have trouble syncing to the current state of the blockchain at all, pointing out some bugs in this early software, as well as issues relating to dependencies and the challenge of using such old clients today (some of which we covered in chapter 4). We then go on to sum up some of the most important performance improvements that have been included in new Bitcoin Core releases over time.

The figure on the next page shows the result of the analysis from 2017.[32]

---

[31]https://blog.lopp.net/bitcoin-core-performance-evolution/

[32]https://sprovoost.nl/2017/07/22/historical-bitcoin-core-client-performance-c5f16e1f8ccb/

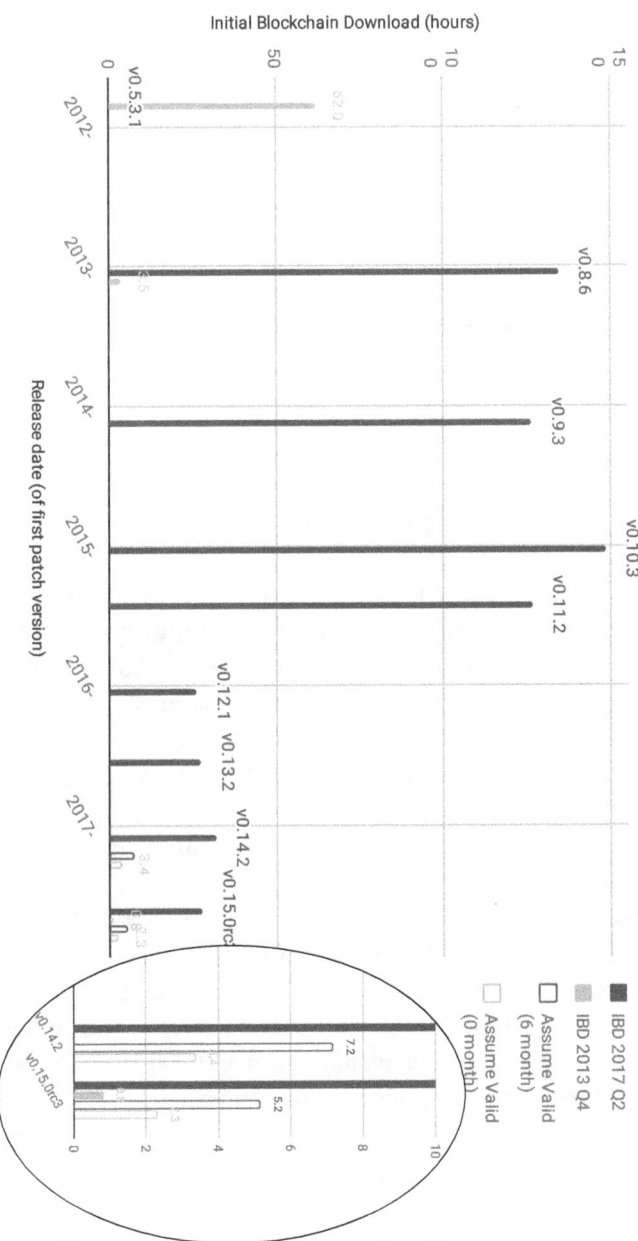

IBD on EC2 (~474K blocks, t2.xlarge, 4 cores, 16 GiB, GP2 200 GiB SSD). We explained Assume Valid in chapter 5.

Appendix B

A Crime on Testnet

This dystopian fiction, which explains the basics of blockchain analytics, was originally published as a blog post.[1]

On a warm summer day I crave a frappuccino. Unfortunately drugs such as caffeine, sugar and cacao were declared illegal decades ago. This happened because young unemployed college graduates often felt triggered by loud caffeinated rich people. Sugar was causing mass obesity and was also a carcinogen. Cacao was too clearly associated with oppression. These days hardly anyone remembers the reasons, they're just shown pictures of cocaine addicts and are told cacao is a gateway drug to that.

Fortunately I know a guy, and he charges 0.002,000,– bitcoin. I spin up my Bitcoin Core wallet, because I like the retro look. It doesn't even use comma's after the decimal separator, something we all got used to during the hyper-deflation era. Some people would just say 2,000 Bitcoin, but don't say that anywhere near a Core church!

---

[1]https://sprovoost.nl/2018/12/28/a-crime-on-testnet-6d95ede8da
03/ ▦

First I need to buy some Bitcoin. Bitcoin in Europe is a bit like guns in the USA. A lot of people don't like it, others love it, but it's perfectly legal. So I surf to bitonic.nl to buy a little more than I need:

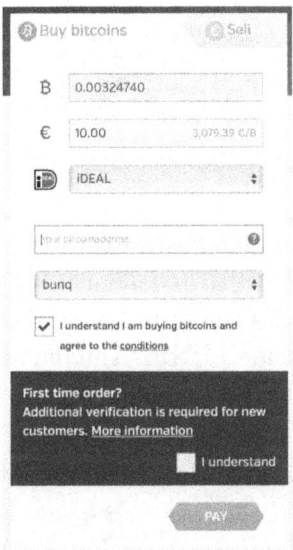

I pay with iDEAL, which is used for all online (fiat) shopping. They need a Bitcoin address to send it to, which I obtain from my Bitcoin Core wallet:

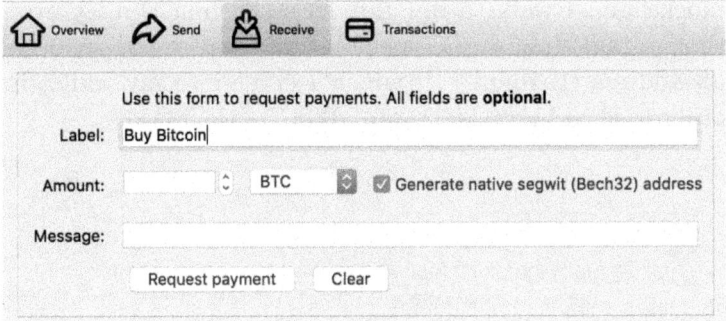

I click Request payment and get an address:

tb1q9jdtpsqxaqd8am70a7g67xn05y9x6dzremuydk

I copy the address into the Bitonic form under "Your bitcoinaddress", ignore all the warnings my banking app gives, and finish the €10 payment. A few moments later Bitcoin Core tells me that I received 0.003,247,40 BTC on the address that I labeled "Buy Bitcoin" and that I gave to Bitonic (tb1q9jdtps...):

Balances		**Recent transactions**	
Available:	0.00324740 BTC	14-12-18 12:36	+0.00324740 BTC
Pending:	0.00000000 BTC	Buy Bitcoin	
Total:	0.00324740 BTC		

While I wait for the transaction to confirm on the blockchain, I walk to my guy, let's call him Dmitry even though that's racist. He opens his own wallet and gives me an address (tb1qnm...), which I enter into my wallet in order to send him 0.0002,000,– BTC.

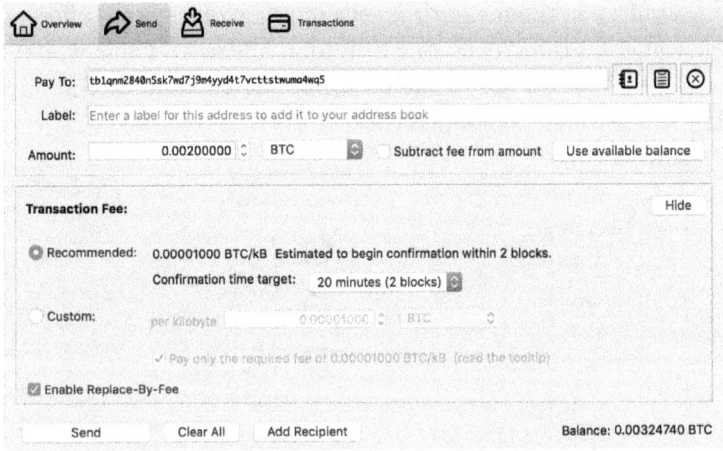

Dmitry knows where I live, so he doesn't wait for confirmation and just gives me the frap. We could have used Lightning to make the payment go through instantly without having to wait for confirmation. Lightning also doesn't leave the same traces on the blockchain, so it could have prevented the pain soon to come. But we didn't.

So now my wallet looks like this and that should be where the story ends for me:

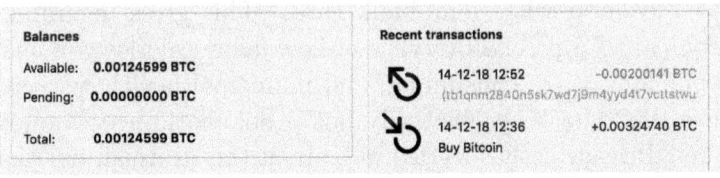

Dmitry in the mean time sells a bunch of fraps to different customers, giving each one a unique address. Their wallets will look exactly the same as mine. At the end of the day, Dmitry's wallet looks like this:

Balances		Recent transactions		
Available:	**0.00400000 BTC**	↘↻	14-12-18 13:15 1x Frap	[+0.00200000 BTC]
Pending:	**0.00200000 BTC**	↘↻	14-12-18 13:02 1x Frap	+0.00200000 BTC
Total:	**0.00600000 BTC**	↘↻	14-12-18 13:00 1x Frap	+0.00200000 BTC

Dmitry wants to buy some alcohol, the only drug that's still legal, despite the violence, broken families, destroyed careers, crime, disease and mass road casualties it caused, especially after AI cars were banned. This was partially because AI cars enriched the big corporations that leased them out to the poor - who previously couldn't afford a car - but what really broke the camels back was the ISIS hack that killed 15 million people during their work commute.

Alcohol is only for sale in supermarkets and in order to monitor population health, you're strongly encouraged to buy food with your bank card. This gives insurance companies a precise overview of how many calories you and your family are consuming, and municipal health workers use this data to pro-actively put problematic people on a diet. Privacy activists cried wolf about this as usual, but the policy never caused any real issues and the health statistics speak for themselves. There was a proposal to allow Bitcoin payments in supermarkets by taking a passport scan, like with cash, but this lead to GDPR problems.

Anyway, why doesn't Dmitry just use Bitonic to sell his coins? Well, because he has a criminal record for selling caffeine and people with criminal records are barred from buying and selling Bitcoin. Enter Kees, the main character in our story. Kees is a Bitcoin trader and he offers to buy Dmitry's coins for 10% below their market price.

So Dmitry now has an empty wallet and Kees received just a little under 0.006,000,– BTC in his wallet (miners take a small fee to process each transaction):

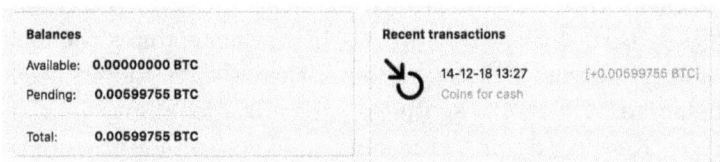

Balances

Available: 0.00000000 BTC

Pending: 0.00599755 BTC

Total: 0.00599755 BTC

Recent transactions

14-12-18 13:27 [+0.00599755 BTC]
Coins for cash

Kees has a problem. He's being watched. Soon after the trade with Dmitry an undercover cop offers to sell 0.001,000,– BTC. Kees offers him cash at 10% below the market price and gives the address tb1q3nf... Now his wallet looks like this:

Balances

Available: 0.00599755 BTC

Pending: 0.00100000 BTC

Total: 0.00699755 BTC

Recent transactions

14-12-18 13:48 [+0.00100000 BTC]
Coins for cash

14-12-18 13:27 +0.00599755 BTC
Coins for cash

Unbeknownst to Kees, Dmitry was caught on camera selling coffee that day, he was arrested on his way out of the supermarket. His (empty) Bitcoin wallet was confiscated, as was his now empty fiat wallet and what was left in the liquor bottle. The wallet contained transactions and notes as you can see above. The timing of each transaction coincided with the camera footage, the amount matched the well known price of fraps, and the notes even said it was fraps. The wallet also shows the destination address where Dmitry sent the BTC (tb1qja...), which the police suspect belongs to Kees. They suspect Dmitry sold the coins in exchange for cash, though they were too late to find the cash.

Kees is not arrested yet and so nobody knows what his Bitcoin addresses are. A privacy activist approaches him, because he wants to buy Bitcoin and doesn't want the kind of surveillance that comes with buying coins online with iDeal. He has no intention of committing any crime whatsoever, not even tax evasion. He withdraws some of his hard and legally earned cash from an ATM. He then endures the long phone interrogation by his bank that always follows such behavior. He then negotiates a nice 3% fee above market rate. Kees sends him the coins, so Kees' wallet now looks like this (2 buys, 1 sell):

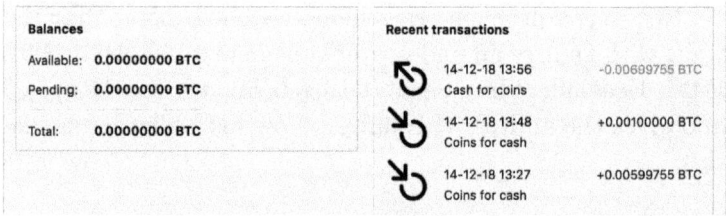

Meanwhile our police officer, let's call him Donald, goes online and looks up the address used in his trade with Kees (tb1q3nf...). Bitcoin Core doesn't support address lookups, because it doesn't scale well and as Wladimir van der Laan put it "bitcoin core is not meant as a chain analysis platform". His favorite block explorer blockchain.com doesn't support bech32 address lookups, so he goes to a competitor.

The figure on the next page describes transactions related to the tb1q3nf... address. He suspects this address belongs to Kees, because it's the address Kees gave him to send coins to.

Reading from bottom to top, at 13:51:15 officer Donald sees coins from his own address (tb1qjy4..., blue) go to this address (again: tb1q3nf..., yellow, the address Kees gave him). He also sees coins going back to his own wallet as change (tb1q80q..., also blue).

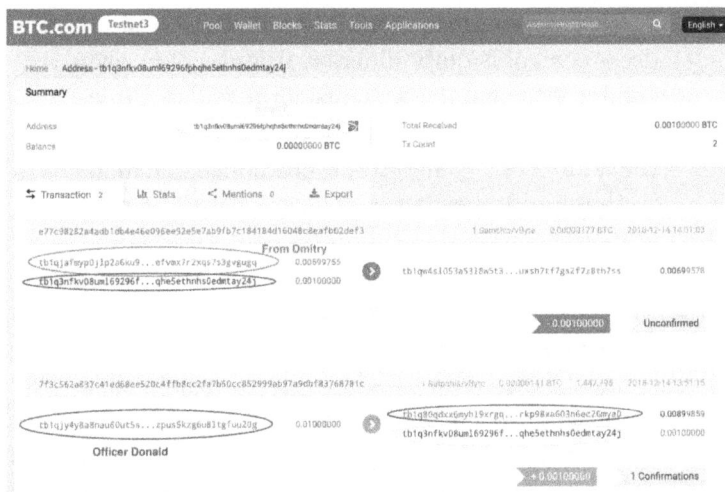

Above, at 14:01:03, he sees his coins (again: tb1q3nf...,
this time blue) combined with coins from Dmitry's wallet
which was confiscated earlier (red). The coins go to some
unknown address (which we know is the privacy activist).

This act of combining coins is crucial. If Kees had sold
the undercover police coins seperate from Dmitry's coins,
there would have been no visible link between them.

Donald picks up a paper written ages ago in 2013 called
A Fistful of Bitcoins, which says the following:[2]

> HEURISTIC 1. If two (or more) addresses are in-
> puts to the same transaction, they are controlled
> by the same user; i.e., for any transaction t, all
> pk E inputs(t) are controlled by the same user.

Well, that looks really scientific! Never mind that a
heuristic is just that, a heuristic, not a fact. In his report,
he also decides to leave out sentences like the following:

---

[2]https://cseweb.ucsd.edu/~smeiklejohn/files/imc13.pdf

Finally, we emphasize that our definition of address control is quite different from account ownership; for example, we consider a wallet service such as Instawallet to be the controller of each of the addresses it generates, even though the funds in these addresses are owned by a wide variety of distinct users.

In this case of course we know the heuristic was correct, because we've seen Kees' wallet. But Kees used encryption and his wallet is safe. He uses his right to remain silent. Not always a wise choice when you're confronted with money laundering charges, because presumption of innocence and the right to remain silent are more or less thrown out the window.

Kees is now charged with laundering 0.007,000,– bitcoin, namely the amount from Donald plus the amount from Dmitry. If the "cluster" that forms his wallet included more transaction, then those would have been added to the total amount as well. Because Donald paid a 10% fee, it is automatically assumed he also charged Kees 10%, and since that is more than Bitonic charges, this - in the opinion of the public prosecutor, should have given Kees sufficient reason to suspect illegal origin of the funds, and thus he should have enquired about them.

The burden of evidence is therefore shifted to Kees and he needs to provide an explanation, one that is not a priori unreasonable, for the origin of the 0.006,000,–. He doesn't, so he's convicted and goes to jail.

This is the simplest case I can think of to demonstrate how cluster analysis works, and how it's actually being used. In practice cases are far more complicated and the analysis isn't done in the fairly thorough way I describe above. Instead, the police relies on companies like Chainalysis to figure out which addresses belong to whom and they produce fancy charts that tell if someone is guilty.

Nobody knows what data sources companies like Chainal-ysis use or how they find clusters; that proprietary evidence is held back. There are countless ways in which these analyses can go wrong, it very quickly leads to cargo cult science[3] and witch trials, with potentially false convictions as a result. Good luck finding defense counsel who understands this, and even more luck explaining this in court (after you've spent a few months in prison without bail).

---

[3]https://en.wikipedia.org/wiki/Cargo_cult_science

Appendix C

Bitcoin White Paper

The following pages contain the Bitcoin white paper. The layout has been modified slightly to be more suitable for a book.

If you prefer to the read the original, you can download it,[1] but there's a more interesting way to get it! In chapter 5 we explained how the unspent transaction output (UTXO) set tracks every coin currently in existence. A coin consists of an amount, plus the script that needs to be satisfied to spend that coin (see e.g. chapter 10).

In place of a real script, it's also possible to stuff a UTXO with completely arbitrary data. In the past, when transaction fees were still very low, many random things were uploaded to the blockchain, including pictures of Nelson Mandela and Barack Obama — and the Bitcoin white paper.[2]

---

[1]https://bitcoin.org/bitcoin.pdf

[2]Sward, A., Vecna, I., & Stonedahl, F. (2018). Data Insertion in Bitcoin's Blockchain. Ledger, 3. https://doi.org/10.5195/ledger.2018. 101

The following command extracts the white paper from the UTXO set[3]:

```
b=54e48e5f5c656b26c3bca14a8c95aa58\
3d07ebe84dde3b7dd4a78f4e4186e713
for ((o=0;o<946;++o))
do bitcoin-cli gettxout $b $o
done | jq -r '.scriptPubKey.asm' |
cut -d' ' -f2-4 |
xxd -r -p |
tail -c+9 |
head -c184292 > bitcoin.pdf
```

You can verify the checksum for this PDF:

```
shasum -a 256 bitcoin.pdf
```

The result should be:

```
b1674191a88ec5cdd733e4240a818031
05dc412d6c6708d53ab94fc248f4f553
```

Because the arbitrary data doesn't correspond to any real public key, these coins can never be spent. Although that follows from common sense, there's no way to mathematically prove it. This means that all nodes have to keep these coins — i.e. the white paper — in memory until the end of time, or until a Utreexo soft fork (chapter 6) removes the need for nodes to store the UTXO set.

---

[3]https://www.reddit.com/r/Bitcoin/comments/l2yu4k/comment/gke25ve/

Bitcoin: A Peer-to-Peer Electronic Cash System

Satoshi Nakamoto

satoshin@gmx.com

www.bitcoin.org

Abstract. A purely peer-to-peer version of electronic cash would allow online payments to be sent directly from one party to another without going through a financial institution. Digital signatures provide part of the solution, but the main benefits are lost if a trusted third party is still required to prevent double-spending. We propose a solution to the double-spending problem using a peer-to-peer network. The network timestamps transactions by hashing them into an ongoing chain of hash-based proof-of-work, forming a record that cannot be changed without redoing the proof-of-work. The longest chain not only serves as proof of the sequence of events witnessed, but proof that it came from the largest pool of CPU power. As long as a majority of CPU power is controlled by nodes that are not cooperating to attack the network, they'll generate the longest chain and outpace attackers. The network itself requires minimal structure. Messages are broadcast on a best effort basis, and nodes can leave and rejoin the network at will, accepting the longest proof-of-work chain as proof of what happened while they were gone.

1. Introduction

Commerce on the Internet has come to rely almost exclusively on financial institutions serving as trusted third parties to process electronic payments. While the system works well enough for most transactions, it still suffers from the inherent weaknesses of the trust based model. Completely non-reversible transactions are not really possible, since financial institutions cannot avoid mediating disputes. The cost of mediation increases transaction costs, limiting the minimum practical transaction size and cutting off the possibility for small casual transactions, and there is a broader cost in the loss of ability to make non-reversible payments for non-reversible services. With the possibility of reversal, the need for trust spreads. Merchants must be wary of their customers, hassling them for more information than they would otherwise need. A certain percentage of fraud is accepted as unavoidable. These costs and payment uncertainties can be avoided in person by using physical currency, but no mechanism exists to make payments over a communications channel without a trusted party.

What is needed is an electronic payment system based on cryptographic proof instead of trust, allowing any two willing parties to transact directly with each other without the need for a trusted third party. Transactions that are computationally impractical to reverse would protect sellers from fraud, and routine escrow mechanisms could easily be implemented to protect buyers. In this paper, we propose a solution to the double-spending problem using a peer-to-peer distributed timestamp server to generate computational proof of the chronological order of transactions. The system is secure as long as honest nodes collectively control more CPU power than any cooperating group of attacker nodes.

2. Transactions

We define an electronic coin as a chain of digital signatures. Each owner transfers the coin to the next by digitally signing a hash of the previous transaction and the public key of the next owner and adding these to the end of the coin. A payee can verify the signatures to verify the chain of ownership.

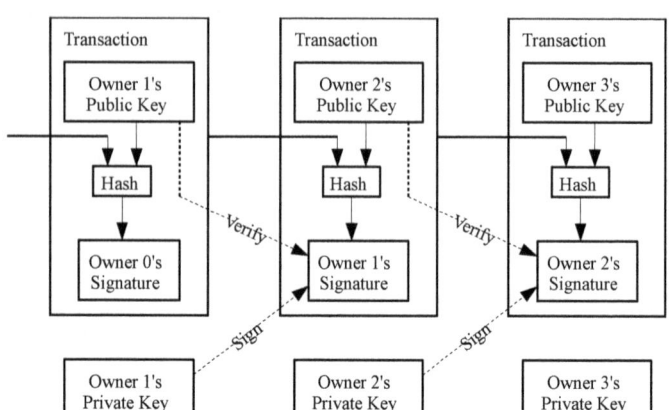

The problem of course is the payee can't verify that one of the owners did not double-spend the coin. A common solution is to introduce a trusted central authority, or mint, that checks every transaction for double spending. After each transaction, the coin must be returned to the mint to issue a new coin, and only coins issued directly from the mint are trusted not to be double-spent. The problem with this solution is that the fate of the entire money system depends on the company running the mint, with every transaction having to go through them, just like a bank.

We need a way for the payee to know that the previous owners did not sign any earlier transactions. For our purposes, the earliest transaction is the one that counts, so we don't care about later attempts to double-spend. The only way to confirm the absence of a transaction is to be aware of all transactions. In the mint based model, the mint was aware of all transactions and decided which arrived first. To accomplish this without a trusted party, transactions must be publicly announced [1], and we need a system for participants to agree on a single history of the order in which they were received. The payee needs proof that at the time of each transaction, the majority of nodes agreed it was the first received.

3. Timestamp Server

The solution we propose begins with a timestamp server. A timestamp server works by taking a hash of a block of items to be timestamped and widely publishing the hash, such as in a newspaper or Usenet post [2-5]. The timestamp proves that the data must have existed at the time, obviously, in order to get into the hash. Each timestamp includes the previous timestamp in its hash, forming a chain, with each additional timestamp reinforcing the ones before it.

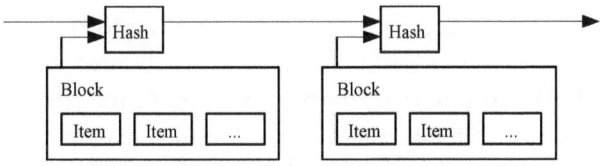

4. Proof-of-Work

To implement a distributed timestamp server on a peer-to-peer basis, we will need to use a proof-of-work system similar to Adam Back's Hashcash [6], rather than newspaper or Usenet posts. The proof-of-work involves scanning for a value that when hashed, such as with SHA-256, the hash begins with a number of zero bits. The average work required is exponential in the number of zero bits required and can be verified by executing a single hash.

For our timestamp network, we implement the proof-of-work by incrementing a nonce in the block until a value is found that gives the block's hash the required zero bits. Once the CPU effort has been expended to make it satisfy the proof-of-work, the block cannot be changed without redoing the work. As later blocks are chained after it, the work to change the block would include redoing all the blocks after it.

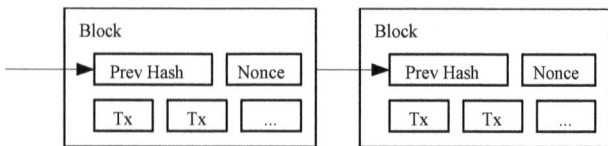

The proof-of-work also solves the problem of determining representation in majority decision making. If the majority were based on one-IP-address-one-vote, it could be subverted by anyone able to allocate many IPs. Proof-of-work is essentially one-CPU-one-vote. The majority decision is represented by the longest chain, which has the greatest proof-of-work effort invested in it. If a majority of CPU power is controlled by honest nodes, the honest chain will grow the fastest and outpace any competing chains. To modify a past block, an attacker would have to redo the proof-of-work of the block and all blocks after it and then catch up with and surpass the work of the honest nodes. We will show later that the probability of a slower attacker catching up diminishes exponentially as subsequent blocks are added.

To compensate for increasing hardware speed and varying interest in running nodes over time, the proof-of-work difficulty is determined by a moving average targeting an average number of blocks per hour. If they're generated too fast, the difficulty increases.

5. Network

The steps to run the network are as follows:

1) New transactions are broadcast to all nodes.
2) Each node collects new transactions into a block.
3) Each node works on finding a difficult proof-of-work for its block.

4) When a node finds a proof-of-work, it broadcasts the block to all nodes.
5) Nodes accept the block only if all transactions in it are valid and not already spent.
6) Nodes express their acceptance of the block by working on creating the next block in the chain, using the hash of the accepted block as the previous hash.

Nodes always consider the longest chain to be the correct one and will keep working on extending it. If two nodes broadcast different versions of the next block simultaneously, some nodes may receive one or the other first. In that case, they work on the first one they received, but save the other branch in case it becomes longer. The tie will be broken when the next proof- of-work is found and one branch becomes longer; the nodes that were working on the other branch will then switch to the longer one.

New transaction broadcasts do not necessarily need to reach all nodes. As long as they reach many nodes, they will get into a block before long. Block broadcasts are also tolerant of dropped messages. If a node does not receive a block, it will request it when it receives the next block and realizes it missed one.

6. Incentive

By convention, the first transaction in a block is a special transaction that starts a new coin owned by the creator of the block. This adds an incentive for nodes to support the network, and provides a way to initially distribute coins into circulation, since there is no central authority to issue them. The steady addition of a constant of amount of new coins is analogous to gold miners expending resources to add gold to circulation. In our case, it is CPU time and electricity that is expended.

The incentive can also be funded with transaction fees. If the output value of a transaction is less than its input value, the difference is a transaction fee that is added to the incentive value of the block containing the transaction. Once a predetermined number of coins have entered circulation, the incentive can transition entirely to transaction fees and be completely inflation free.

The incentive may help encourage nodes to stay honest. If a greedy attacker is able to assemble more CPU power than all the honest nodes, he would have to choose between using it to defraud people by stealing back his payments, or using it to generate new coins. He ought to find it more profitable to play by the rules, such rules that favour him with more new coins than everyone else combined, than to undermine the system and the validity of his own wealth.

7. Reclaiming Disk Space

Once the latest transaction in a coin is buried under enough blocks, the spent transactions before it can be discarded to save disk space. To facilitate this without breaking the block's hash, transactions are hashed in a Merkle Tree [7][2][5], with only the root included in the block's hash. Old blocks can then be compacted by stubbing off branches of the tree. The interior hashes do not need to be stored.

A block header with no transactions would be about 80 bytes. If we suppose blocks are generated every 10 minutes, 80 bytes * 6 * 24 * 365 = 4.2MB per year. With computer systems typically selling with 2GB of RAM as of 2008, and Moore's Law predicting current growth of 1.2GB per year, storage should not be a problem even if the block headers must be kept in memory.

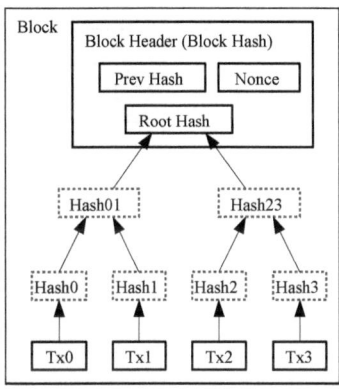

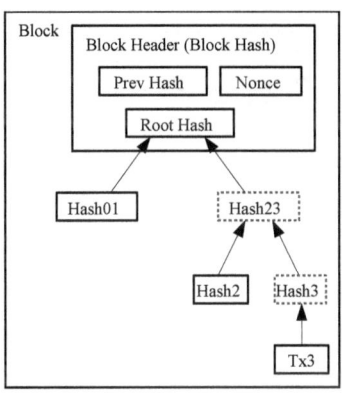

Transactions Hashed in a Merkle Tree   After Pruning Tx0-2 from the Block

8. Simplified Payment Verification

It is possible to verify payments without running a full network node. A user only needs to keep a copy of the block headers of the longest proof-of-work chain, which he can get by querying network nodes until he's convinced he has the longest chain, and obtain the Merkle branch linking the transaction to the block it's timestamped in. He can't check the transaction for himself, but by linking it to a place in the chain, he can see that a network node has accepted it, and blocks added after it further confirm the network has accepted it.

As such, the verification is reliable as long as honest nodes control the network, but is more vulnerable if the network is overpowered by an attacker. While network nodes can verify transactions for themselves, the simplified method can be fooled by an attacker's fabricated transactions for as long as the attacker can continue to overpower the network. One strategy to protect against this would be to accept alerts from network nodes when they detect an invalid block, prompting the user's software to download the full block and alerted transactions to confirm the inconsistency. Businesses

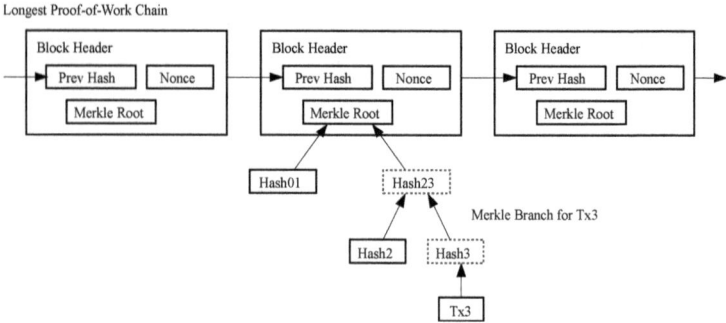

that receive frequent payments will probably still want to run their own nodes for more independent security and quicker verification.

9. Combining and Splitting Value

Although it would be possible to handle coins individually, it would be unwieldy to make a separate transaction for every cent in a transfer. To allow value to be split and combined, transactions contain multiple inputs and outputs. Normally there will be either a single input from a larger previous transaction or multiple inputs combining smaller amounts, and at most two outputs: one for the payment, and one returning the change, if any, back to the sender.

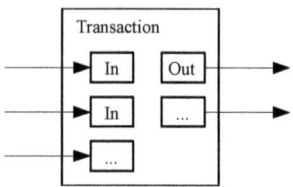

It should be noted that fan-out, where a transaction depends on several transactions, and those transactions depend on many more, is not a problem here. There is never the need to extract a complete standalone copy of a transaction's history.

10. Privacy

The traditional banking model achieves a level of privacy by limiting access to information to the parties involved and the trusted third party. The necessity to announce all transactions publicly precludes this method, but privacy can still be maintained by breaking the flow of information in another place: by keeping public keys anonymous. The public can see that someone is sending an amount to someone else, but without information linking the transaction to anyone. This is similar to the level of information released by stock exchanges, where the time and size of individual trades, the "tape", is made public, but without telling who the parties were.

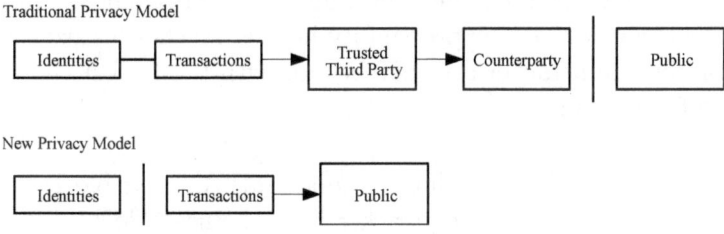

As an additional firewall, a new key pair should be used for each transaction to keep them from being linked to a common owner. Some linking is still unavoidable with multi-input transactions, which necessarily reveal that their inputs were owned by the same owner. The risk is that if the owner of a key is revealed, linking could reveal other transactions that belonged to the same owner.

11. Calculations

We consider the scenario of an attacker trying to generate an alternate chain faster than the honest chain. Even if this is accomplished, it does not throw the system open to arbitrary changes, such as creating value out of thin air or taking money that never belonged to the attacker. Nodes are not going to accept an invalid transaction as payment, and honest nodes will never accept a block containing them. An attacker can only try to change one of his own transactions to take back money he recently spent.

The race between the honest chain and an attacker chain can be characterized as a Binomial Random Walk. The success event is the honest chain being extended by one block, increasing its lead by +1, and the failure event is the attacker's chain being extended by one block, reducing the gap by -1.

The probability of an attacker catching up from a given deficit is analogous to a Gambler's Ruin problem. Suppose a gambler with unlimited credit starts at a deficit and plays potentially an infinite number of trials to try to reach breakeven. We can calculate the probability he ever reaches breakeven, or that an attacker ever catches up with the honest chain, as follows [8]:

p = probability an honest node finds the next block
q = probability the attacker finds the next block
q_z = probability the attacker will ever catch up from z blocks behind

$$q_z = \left\{ \begin{array}{ll} 1 & \text{if } p \le q \\ (q/p)^z & \text{if } p > q \end{array} \right\}$$

Given our assumption that p > q, the probability drops exponentially as the number of blocks the attacker has to catch up with increases. With the odds against him, if he doesn't make a lucky lunge forward early on, his chances become vanishingly small as he falls further behind.

We now consider how long the recipient of a new transaction needs to wait before being sufficiently certain the sender can't change the transaction. We assume the sender is an attacker who wants to make the recipient believe he paid him for a while, then switch it to pay back to himself after some time has passed. The receiver will be alerted when that happens, but the sender hopes it will be too late.

The receiver generates a new key pair and gives the public key to the sender shortly before signing. This prevents the sender from preparing a chain of blocks ahead of time by working on it continuously until he is lucky enough to get far enough ahead, then executing the transaction at that moment. Once the transaction is sent, the dishonest sender starts working in secret on a parallel chain containing an alternate version of his transaction.

The recipient waits until the transaction has been added to a block and z blocks have been linked after it. He doesn't know the exact amount of progress the attacker has made, but assuming the honest blocks took the average expected time per block, the attacker's potential progress will be a Poisson distribution with expected value:

$$\lambda = z\frac{q}{p}$$

To get the probability the attacker could still catch up now, we multiply the Poisson density for each amount of progress he could have made by the probability he could catch up from that point:

$$\sum_{k=0}^{\infty} \frac{\lambda^k e^{-\lambda}}{k!} \cdot \left\{ \begin{array}{ll} (q/p)^{(z-k)} & \text{if } k \leq z \\ 1 & \text{if } k > z \end{array} \right\}$$

Rearranging to avoid summing the infinite tail of the distribution...

$$1 - \sum_{k=0}^{z} \frac{\lambda^k e^{-\lambda}}{k!} \left(1 - (q/p)^{(z-k)} \right)$$

Converting to C code...

```c
#include <math.h>
double AttackerSuccessProbability(double q, int z)
{
    double p = 1.0 - q;
    double lambda = z * (q / p);
    double sum = 1.0;
    int i, k;
    for (k = 0; k <= z; k++)
    {
        double poisson = exp(-lambda);
        for (i = 1; i <= k; i++)
            poisson *= lambda / i;
        sum -= poisson * (1 - pow(q / p, z - k));
    }
    return sum;
}
```

Running some results, we can see the probability drop off exponentially with z.

```
q=0.1
z=0    P=1.0000000
z=1    P=0.2045873
z=2    P=0.0509779
z=3    P=0.0131722
z=4    P=0.0034552
z=5    P=0.0009137
z=6    P=0.0002428
z=7    P=0.0000647
z=8    P=0.0000173
```

```
z=9     P=0.0000046
z=10    P=0.0000012

q=0.3
z=0     P=1.0000000
z=5     P=0.1773523
z=10    P=0.0416605
z=15    P=0.0101008
z=20    P=0.0024804
z=25    P=0.0006132
z=30    P=0.0001522
z=35    P=0.0000379
z=40    P=0.0000095
z=45    P=0.0000024
z=50    P=0.0000006
```

Solving for P less than 0.1%...

```
P < 0.001
q=0.10    z=5
q=0.15    z=8
q=0.20    z=11
q=0.25    z=15
q=0.30    z=24
q=0.35    z=41
q=0.40    z=89
q=0.45    z=340
```

12. Conclusion

We have proposed a system for electronic transactions without relying on trust. We started with the usual framework of coins made from digital signatures, which provides strong control of ownership, but is incomplete without a way to prevent double-spending. To solve this, we proposed a peer-to-peer network using proof-of-work to record a public history of transactions that quickly becomes computationally impractical for an attacker to change if honest nodes control a majority of CPU power. The network is robust in its unstructured simplicity. Nodes work all at once with little coordination. They do not need to be identified, since messages are not routed to any particular place and only need to be delivered on a best effort basis. Nodes can leave and rejoin the network at will, accepting the proof-of-work chain as proof of what happened while they were gone. They vote with their CPU power, expressing their acceptance of valid blocks by working on extending them and rejecting invalid blocks by refusing to work on them. Any needed rules and incentives can be enforced with this consensus mechanism.

References

[1] W. Dai, "b-money," http://www.weidai.com/bmoney. txt ▨, 1998.

[2] H. Massias, X.S. Avila, and J.-J. Quisquater, "Design of a secure timestamping service with minimal trust requirements," In 20th Symposium on Information Theory in the Benelux, May 1999.

[3] S. Haber, W.S. Stornetta, "How to time-stamp a digital document," In Journal of Cryptology, vol 3, no 2, pages 99-111, 1991.

[4] D. Bayer, S. Haber, W.S. Stornetta, "Improving the efficiency and reliability of digital time-stamping," In Sequences II: Methods in Communication, Security and Computer Science, pages 329-334, 1993.

[5] S. Haber, W.S. Stornetta, "Secure names for bit-strings," In Proceedings of the 4th ACM Conference on Computer and Communications Security, pages 28-35, April 1997.

[6] A. Back, "Hashcash - a denial of service countermeasure," http://www.hashcash.org/papers/hashcash.pdf ▨, 2002.

[7] R.C. Merkle, "Protocols for public key cryptosystems," In Proc. 1980 Symposium on Security and Privacy, IEEE Computer Society, pages 122-133, April 1980.

[8] W. Feller, "An introduction to probability theory and its applications," 1957.